Mt. Rainier & South Cascades Fishing Guide

Mt. Rainier National Park and South Cascade Mountain Lakes & Streams

By Dave Shorett

ISBN: 0-9652116-1-4

Library of Congress Catalog Card Number: 98-091474

Publisher: Lakestream Publications, 200 Maynard Building, 119 1st Avenue South, Seattle, WA. Phone: (206) 842-9202.

Page layout: Charles B. Summers, Pacific Publication Services, P. O. Box H, South Bend, WA 98586. Phone: (360) 875-6091.

Maps: Jim Singer, 13215 118th Avenue N. E., Kirkland, WA 98034.

Photograph Credits: U. S. National Park Service, pages 7, 11, 18, 43, 45, 58; U. S. National Forest Service, pages 52, 54, 55, 66, 69, 75, 80, 82; Washington Department of Fish & Wildlife, pages 17, 89, 91, 97, 100, 106, 108, 112, 114, 123, 124, 125, 131. All other photos by the author, except where designated otherwise.

Acknowledgments

I want to thank the following persons for their assistance in making this book possible: Ted Lloyd, Eric Anderson, Jim Cummins, Terry Lawson, Ken Meyer, Jack Thorne, Barbara Samora, Cy Hentges, Bob Dopiriak, Mike Rowan, Tim Lofgren, Barry Olson, Charles Summers, Jim Singer, Julie Jones, John Weinheimer, Chris Axling, and Peter Shorett.

I wish to give special thanks to Stan Jones, who died February 25, 1997, at age 74. Stan was the author and publisher of five books on fishing, including seven editions of the *Washington State Fishing Guide*. He also wrote many articles for outdoor publications, held editorial positions with *Fishing and Hunting News* and the *Alaska Sportsman,* and served many years as Executive Director for the Northwest Outdoor Writers' Association.

Stan spent many hours with me, encouraging and actively helping me write this book. Through his books, he introduced practically all the author's generation of anglers to fishing in Washington. He knew, as is becoming increasingly evident, that without inspired anglers to act as advocates for the environment, habitat would be degraded and disappear, leaving the state's fish populations unprotected and in a state of demise. I hope that at least a few anglers, if not many, through reading this guidebook and fishing these waters, will become informed and passionate enough about fishing and the environment to become advocates for our state's fish.

Table of Contents

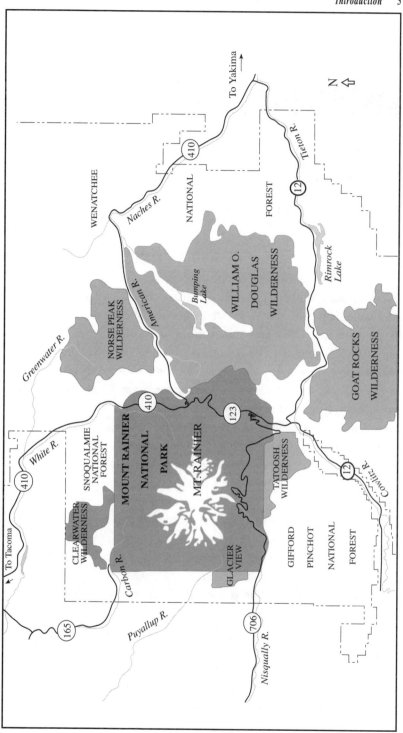

Introduction

When the God of the Outdoors created Washington's Cascade Range. . . he scattered hundreds of mountain lakes amid their towering peaks. These crystal clear basins of water are set like sapphires and emeralds amid the snow fields and tree-clad rocks. . . .

Enos Bradner

Mt. Rainier National Park lies approximately in the middle of Washington's southern Cascade mountain range. It was created in 1899, the fifth National Park established in the United States. The Park comprises 378 square miles and contains more than 250 lakes and over 400 streams. The surrounding Wilderness, National Forest, and privately held areas encompass a greater number of lakes and streams. Some lakes, particularly in the Park, and a few streams, do not contain trout or simply have fish which are too small to be worth the effort, but on the whole, this region has plenty of lakes and streams that provide quality angling experiences.

Mount Rainier itself, known in the Puget Sound region simply as "the mountain," is visible from a distance of more than 100 miles in clear weather. At 14,411 feet, it is the highest volcano and has the largest mass in the Cascade Range. To understand its geology, ecology and weather, learning a few things about it is important: it is very steep, in approximately seven miles rising nearly 11,000 feet from its base to its summit; it contains the largest single peak glacier system in the lower 48 states; holds the United States records for average snowfall, 575 inches, and one year's snowfall, 93 feet; and claims the world's largest mudflow. It also creates its own weather system.

Anglers visiting Mt. Rainier National Park must be aware that melt-off, on lakes and particularly as it affects streams, is a most important consideration. Melt-off limits fishing in all lakes, most of the Park's lakes being iced-over until at least June, many into July and some into August. Glaciers which produce "rock flour," rock ground up to the point where it becomes powder, feed many rivers and streams. This flour gives the streams a gray-brown color during most of the summer. All but two of the Park's major rivers are resultantly turbid, except at those times when the weather is cold enough for long enough to clear the water.

Anglers also need to know that many of Mt. Rainier's streams descend steeply down the sides of the mountain, making for few long runs and holding water, lots of plunge pools, and cloudy water conditions during periods of significant rainfall.

Mt. Rainier National Park is bounded on all sides by extensive forested areas, the vast majority of which are publicly owned. To the north lie portions of Mt. Baker-Snoqualmie National Forest, the Clearwater Wilderness area and privately owned forest; on the west, a small part of Mt. Baker-Snoqualmie National Forest, considerable private forest land, the small Glacier View Wilderness, and a modest portion of Gifford Pinchot National Forest; on the south, extensive tracts of Gifford Pinchot National Forest, Tattoosh Wilderness, and

Mt. Rainier National Park Stream.

Goat Rocks Wilderness; and on the east, Wenatchee National Forest, Norse Peak Wilderness, which border the Park on the north as well, and the William O. Douglas Wilderness, itself nearly equal in size to the Park. Together with Mt. Rainier National Park, the entire forested lands give the angler more than 600 square miles of area to fish. To the south of this region lie another many miles of the south Cascade mountains, extending into Oregon.

The effects of urbanization and suburban growth are rapidly encroaching upon Mt. Rainier National Park and the South Cascades. Increased numbers of visitors have resulted in restrictions being imposed upon access, hiking, camping, and fishing. Such restrictions also result from negligence and lack of care for the environment, both inside and outside the Park. If dedicated anglers want to continue fishing this area, they must take to heart the "no-trace" ethic discussed in this book. In essence, the ethic requires that to the very best of our abilities, we leave no trace when we hike, camp or fish, that we are always mindful of what this magnificent environment allows us and we do nothing to endanger it. From a strictly pragmatic point of view, if we do degrade the environment of this area, we will soon lose the opportunity to fish here. For dedicated anglers, that ought to be enough reason. More importantly though, we owe it to ourselves, our children, and all species simply to care for the planet.

How to use this book

This book is an attempt to supply anglers the information they need and can most effectively use to fish for trout in this grand area. It is primarily addressed to fly anglers, but will be equally useful for spin fishermen and parents getting their children started fishing. A brief section introduces Mt. Rainier and South Cascade stream and lake fishing for trout. The region is then divided into North, West, South and East sections. Within each section, the lakes and streams of the south Cascade mountains and those of Mt. Rainier National Park lying within that section are described. Access, species and size of fish and fishing conditions are discussed for each lake and stream. Lakes and streams within Mt. Rainier National Park are designated "(RNP)" throughout the book.

Mt. Rainier and South Cascade Trout

This guidebook attempts to conservatively describe the numbers and size of the region's lake and stream trout populations, based upon actual experience, angler reports and biologists' surveys. Lake populations vary considerably more than stream populations from year to year due to stocking policies, fishing pressure and environmental factors. Accordingly, the descriptions in this guidebook may differ to some extent from what the angler finds in any given year.

There are five species of "trout" in Mt. Rainier National Park and the South Cascade mountains. Rainbow, cutthroat, and browns are true trout. Bull trout and eastern brook are actually chars. Whitefish are also widespread and are related to the salmonids. The following drawings of trout and whitefish were done by Jim Singer.

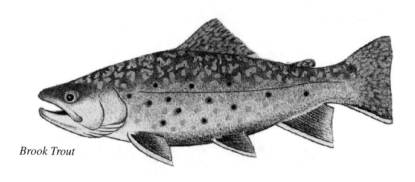

Brook Trout

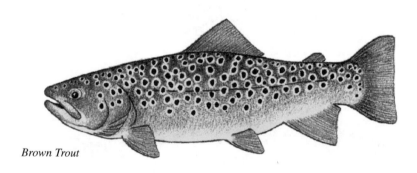

Brown Trout

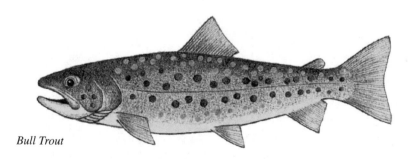

Bull Trout

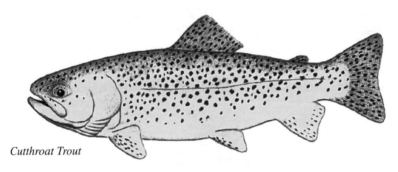

Cutthroat Trout

Rainbow Trout

Whitefish

Access

The maps provided in this guidebook are intended to give accurate directions but are not drawn to scale. Road numbers, description, mileage, specific hiking directions and trail mileage are as accurate as possible. All are subject to change, particularly road numbers. (Sometimes it seems the Forest Service changes the road numbers every year.) Additionally, Forest Service roads are periodically washed out, blocked off, closed and reopened. The only way to be certain of road access is to obtain a current forest service map and inquire at the nearest Ranger station. Topographic maps are indispensable in finding many of the waters described, and anglers are advised to use the best topographic maps and hiking guidebooks available. No one hiking off trail in seach of a lake or stream should think of doing so without such maps, guidebooks, and compass. A list of guidebooks and topopgraphic maps is found in the appendix.

Following the descriptions of the region's lakes and streams, the best fishing techniques are described, followed by an appendix setting forth regulations, license information, campgrounds and other useful information.

Lower Palisades Lake, Mt. Rainier National Park.

Fishing Mt. Rainier & South Cascades

As I held the twisting, struggling fellow in my left hand, my body tingled. I felt the struggle even in my toes. Here was a champion, a fighting heart if ever there was one. He was clean and sleek and committed to life. I could not kill him. He desired life as much as I and was not badly hooked. I returned him to the water.

William O. Douglas

Mt. Rainier National Park Lakes and Streams

Twenty-five lakes are known with certainty to contain trout in Mt. Rainier National Park. There are surely others, a few of which are known primarily to Park employees. Most likely, these will remain well-guarded secrets. Within Park boundaries there are 5 major rivers and at least 15 creeks with substantial trout populations.

Beginning in 1915, the lakes and streams of the Park were regularly planted with trout until 1972, when the National Park Service made a policy decision to cease stocking the Park's lakes and streams. In keeping with the emphasis upon maintaining and restoring natural ecosystems, it was decreed that introducing species of any kind, plant or animal, was to be ended. The trout anglers catch in the Park's streams now are descendants of both native and planted trout and have established their populations in what seem perpetual self-sustaining numbers. Trout inhabiting the lakes are self-sustaining populations descended from planted ancestor stock.

Lakes

Historically, none of the Park's lakes were known to hold trout before stocking, which began as early as 1915. Once they were stocked, some trout populations were able to reproduce successfully. By far the most successful species was the eastern brook. Habitats within lakes, particularly the near shore areas, provide spawning environment used by brook trout and allow their eggs to incubate successfully. With rare exceptions, such as apparently some springs and rarely found substrates, lakes do not afford rainbow and cutthroat the kind of habitat they need to spawn effectively and reproduce. They rely upon inlet and outlet streams. Some lakes have no inlet or outlet stream, many afford no access to such streams where they do exist, and some streams have no suitable spawning habitat. All trout species can spawn in the gravel of streams connected to lakes but rainbow and cutthroat have a significant disadvantage compared to brook trout. Both these species spawn in the spring when the water is high, allowing them to enter the streams and deposit their eggs. If the stream dries up or becomes too dewatered over the summer, the eggs cannot survive to allow fry to hatch. In contrast, brook trout spawn in the fall, as the rains begin and their fertilized eggs are provided the flow necessary to allow fry to hatch in the springtime and survive.

Trout rising on an un-named pond in Mt. Rainier National Park.

Brook trout are then, far more successful in establishing themselves as self-sustaining populations in mountain lakes. This has certainly been the case in Mt. Rainier National Park. In fact, some attempts to remove them from Park lakes have been unsuccessful, as one will note when visiting the Reflection Lakes during a summer evening, when brook trout are happily rising and splashing about, despite an effort to eliminate them from the lake sometime ago. (However, the Park Service has successfully removed fish from some lakes using gill nets and is studying fish removal as part of restoring natural processes and non-fish native species to some lakes) Lake trout populations within the Park are thus primarily eastern brook, and there is only a handful of self-sustaining cutthroat and rainbow lakes, some of which have brook trout as well. These cutthroat and rainbow lakes are rare. Anglers must treat their spawning inlet and outlet streams with extreme caution and not fish them if these trout are to continue to exist in the Park's lakes.

Streams

In contrast to the Park's lakes, a substantial number of its rivers and creeks were known, before any stocking was done, to support native cutthroat, bull trout and in some streams, rainbow trout and mountain whitefish. Before dams were built, on several rivers, there were anadromous fish, salmon, steelhead, sea-run cutthroat and sea-run bull trout which migrated from the Park's streams out to sea and returned to spawn. Some cutthroat, rainbow and bull trout in these streams are descendants of populations which were blocked from migrating out by dams and residualized, migrating up and downstream but not to sea. Other populations in various creeks may have become nonmigratory due to geological changes blocking migration to salt water and have existed as landlocked populations ever since.

The native trout were joined by rainbow, cutthroat, and brook trout raised in hatcheries and planted in the Park's streams over time. Plants varied in frequency and numbers but nearly all of the creeks and rivers in Mt. Rainier National Park were stocked with trout at one time or another until 1972. Different strains of rainbow and cutthroat were also planted from time to time. One of the most frequently found in the streams is the Montana Black Spot, a nonnative cutthroat still thriving in some parts of the Park. Stocked trout found enough success in reproducing that they established populations, the progeny of which survive and, along with native trout, provide enjoyable stream fishing throughout the Park. Hybridization also apparently occurred, as anglers have caught trout resembling "cuttbows," a cross between rainbow and cutthroat, as well as cutthroat which have a different appearance from known strains. Bull trout are also known to hybridize with brook trout.

South Cascade Lakes and Streams

The South Cascade Mountain lakes and streams outside Mt. Rainier National Park have been managed differently from those in the Park.

Greenwater River.

Streams

Many streams outside the Park boundaries were planted with put and take hatchery trout well into the 1990's. This policy is probably at its end with budget cuts, and the advent of a much stronger angler constituency advocating reduced limits, gear restrictions, increased catch and release, and habitat protection for wild trout. While generally, reduced stocking has been accompanied by reduced limits and gear restrictions, for example, an 8 inch minimum size and no use of bait in many streams, too many anglers continue to harvest trout from Washington's streams as though they were still being stocked. This has resulted in substantial reductions in self-sustaining trout populations in the most popular streams. Washington State has historically been slow to protect its wild trout but is beginning to make significant progress. Nevertheless, it is the author's belief that Washington State must move quickly and forcefully to protect wild trout in the Cascade mountain streams by further restricting limits and gear, requiring catch and release in large stretches of most streams and insisting upon habitat protection. In doing so, Washington will catch up with Montana, Idaho, Oregon and California, which have for the most part taken these steps long ago.

Many Cascade streams can and do provide plentiful numbers of trout, particularly in the areas which require walking to reach. Cascade trout seldom reach the average size found in Idaho or Montana, but if the angler is content to spend a day with lots of beautiful, wild, generally small trout rising to a fly, he or she will enjoy the experience of fishing the streams of this area.

There is little reason to keep trout from Cascade streams unless hiking in a considerable distance and staying overnight. Even then, fishermen should be very judicious in the number they kill for food. While the author has found a number of streams are inhabited by abundant, healthy trout, until recently very few studies have been done of the Cascade streams and there is limited scientific information about trout populations in these rivers and creeks. It is recommended that anglers practice catch and release and restrict the use of bait to children learning to fish, and then only where it is not prohibited. (Even the most dyed-in-the-wool fly fishermen recognize the importance of catching fish in initiating youngsters to the difficulty and wonders of stream fishing for trout.)

Lakes

In contrast to the limited scientific information on resident trout in Cascade streams, the area's high mountain lakes have been thoroughly studied. Washington State Department of Fish and Wildlife biologists have visited and quite thoroughly studied virtually every high lake in the South Cascade region surrounding Mount Rainier National Park and regularly revisit them for study, as budgets allow. An effective management policy has been developed from the studies.

Lakes which have self-sustaining populations of trout are not

South Cascade Lake cutthroat.

planted, as a general rule. Brook trout are stocked in very few mountain lakes. Brookies have become self-sustaining in nearly every lake in which they have been planted in the Cascades. Occasionally, the Department will supplement them in a lake with plants of rainbow or cutthroat, but only rarely. The Department basically leaves the brookie lakes alone because unless there is very limited spawning habitat or frequent winter kill, brook trout tend to become small and stunted due to overpopulation, particularly in lakes which do not receive much fishing pressure. In a few lakes, the Department has planted brown trout to prey on the brook trout. There has been excellent success in some cases using this method, resulting in very large brown trout and cropping of the brookie population.

It seems literally impossible to fish out a mountain brookie lake. If the Park Service cannot accomplish this with electro-fishing and gill netting, anglers certainly can't do it with hook and line. Brookie lakes are great places to take kids and beginning anglers, keep a few fish and eat them for dinner and breakfast. Mountain brook trout are unsurpassed at mealtime.

Some Cascade lakes have adequate spawning streams and habitat for cutthroat and rainbow to reproduce in sufficient numbers to ensure self-sustaining numbers of trout year after year. If numbers are sufficient and fishing pressure does not endanger continued existence of trout in a lake, the Department essentially watches the situation but does not intervene. Gear restrictions and reduced limits or catch and release restrictions are sometimes imposed in such lakes, but more often reserved for those lakes which have particularly fragile populations of limited numbers of reproducing cutthroat or rainbow. Occasionally, the Department will supplement these self-sustaining trout with planted cutthroat or rainbow.

In the mid 1970s, the State of Washington, after considerable study, revised the numbers of trout it stocked in mountain lakes. Too often, it was found that when very high numbers of trout were planted in these lakes the result was too many small trout and virtually no large trout. Gradually, the Department developed calculations of the productivity of each lake and optimal numbers of trout to plant to yield lower numbers of trout but of considerably larger size. Anglers were generally pleased with the results and the Department has re-fined this aspect of stocking to the point where it can, in the absence of unpredictable environmental factors, largely determine numbers and size of trout in most mountain lakes which it stocks. Certainly, trout populations will vary significantly from year to year depending upon a host of factors but it is safe to say that the Department's stock-ing policies have greatly enhanced trout fishing in the Cascade lakes.

Much of the high lake stocking is accomplished with the help of volunteers, working with the State, packing the fish in on their backs as fry. Additionally, some high lake fishing clubs have been known to stock high lakes on their own.

Dewey Lakes in South Cascades.

North

I am convinced that the best trout fishing in the United States is in the mountain lakes of the West. It is the best from any standpoint—from numbers of fish, if you want to catch a lot; from the size of the fish, if you want to catch big ones; from the ease with which you can catch them in some lakes, and from the difficulty of fooling the smart lunkers in other lakes if you prefer angling with a challenge.

Ted Trueblood

White River

White River

A large river, fast flowing and generally very milky, the White River is accessible from Enumclaw upstream of Mud Mountain Dam, through the small burg of Greenwater, then is closely paralleled by Highway 410 to the turnoff to Sunrise. The river is virtually unfishable during runoff, which occurs most of the summer. The only time the river clears at all during fishing season is at times in the spring and fall when there are enough freezing nights, with the result that the river clears some. Even then, fishing is very tough, subsurface fishing is the norm and dry fly fishing is seldom productive.

The river has rainbow, cutthroat, brook trout, whitefish and bull trout. Special rules protect the bull trout, as they are endangered. Do not attempt to catch them. Bait fishing should be prohibited in this river to assure the continued existence of the bull trout.

There are anglers who claim to know how and where to fish this river successfully, using spinners and wet flies, generally streamers. There are sizable rainbow to 16 inches, but fishing is very difficult for those who don't have the special knowledge developed and guarded by veteran local fishermen.

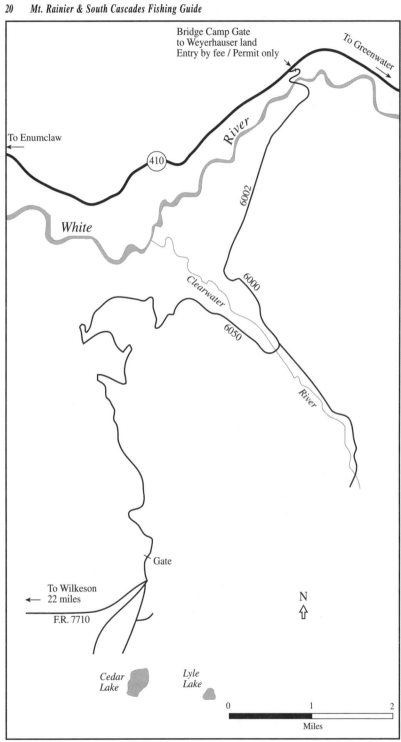

Weyerhaeuser Co. Land

Approximately 5 miles south of Federation Forest State Park, Weyerhaeuser Rd. 6000 crosses the White River and provides access to the Clearwater River and two lakes. Several years ago, the Weyerhaeuser Company decided to limit access to its lands to prevent increasingly severe problems resulting from dumping and vandalism. They established a fee system for entry to its gated areas. One can still walk into those areas but to do any serious fishing or hiking, you will have to buy a pass to gain entry. Entry times are set by a schedule, and regulations must be followed. Inquiry at any Weyerhaeuser office will give you the information needed. A good map is a necessity to navigate the logging roads effectively. A permit will allow access to all of Weyerhaeuser's permit areas, and while of limited use in the South Cascade region, there are many lakes and streams which provide good fishing in Weyerhaeuser's Snoqualmie area.

Clearwater River

The Clearwater river flows entirely on Weyerhaeuser land. The Bridge Camp Weyerhaeuser access gate is found on the right-hand side of Highway 410, after passing the Grass Mountain entry gate on the left. Recreational maps may be obtained at Weyerhaeuser White River facility or at sporting goods stores. From the Bridge Camp entry, follow the main road, Rd. 6000, which turns right onto Rd. 6050 and crosses the river 4.4 miles from the gate. Spur roads lead to the Clearwater along the way to the bridge. Above this bridge Rd. 6041 follows the river through a flat stretch of approximately 0.5 miles and splits to Rd. 6000, which follows the river, crossing it quickly shortly traveling high above the river. From this point upstream, the river is essentially inaccessible except through steep downhill climbing. Surveys have found fair numbers of trout in this area, diminishing as the gradient radically steepens.

The river is best fished from the mouth of the Clearwater where it enters the White River, upstream to the bridge. The river is low gradient and holes are spaced quite far apart. Each hole that is knee-deep or deeper, holds a trout or two, the largest perhaps 11-12 inches. There are lots of salmon fry in this river and they will persistently knock down a dry fly. Nevertheless, the bigger trout will still come up and get it. It is likely that many of the trout vacate this stream as it starts to drop to its lowest levels, and fishing the river is most productive beginning about the middle of July through the middle of August. By mid-September the flow in the river reduces to creek-size.

Cedar Lake (4200)

Popular 36 acre Cedar Lake features an island. There is a small pond to the east and three more over the hill to the south, the smallest draining into Cedar. All may be worth exploring. The shortest route to the lake, but not very short, is through Weyerhaeuser land at the Bridge Camp access gate. After 13 miles on Rd. 6050 you will reach a gate, go through it, take the first left up the hill to the ridge, as far as you can reasonably travel in your vehicle. The lake lies below and can be reached by a well-beaten path that descends along the ridge approximately 300-400 feet to the end of a very rough Weyerhaeuser logging road. From there, a short distance on that road leads to the right and then immediately into the woods and 0.3 miles to the lake. The spur road that takes you to the trail down to the lake can also be reached by traveling forest Rd. 2710 from Wilkeson, approximately 23 miles.

The lake is full of small brookies to approximately 10 inches. In the fall, the brookies take on brilliant spawning colors and are very

Cedar Lake.

easy to catch. This is a good place to bring novice anglers because there are abundant numbers of small brookies and they like to cruise close to shore to feed. A dry fly, such as a small Royal Wulf, Gray Wulf, or Adams will draw strikes even for those who cannot cast very far. The only limitation on bringing novice fishermen is that the trail is quite steep and can be very slippery when it is wet.

Lyle Lake (4150)

This 9 acre, deep lake, drains to the Clearwater River. It lies 4,000 feet east of Cedar Lake and contains eastern brook. Map and compass are necessary to find this seldom visited lake.

Greenwater

As Highway 410 continues past the town of Greenwater, it enters an area where the Weyerhaeuser Co. owns much of the forest land. A permit is required to enter some of this land and access is controlled and changed from time to time. Thus, a telephone call to Weyerhaeuser before planning a trip is a good idea.

Greenwater River

Formerly heavily planted with trout, the lovely Greenwater River flows into the White River at the town of Greenwater. Much of the lower river is bounded by private property and is inaccessible. A few miles toward Chinook Pass from Greenwater, Rd. 70 leads off Highway 410 to several miles of access to the river before deadending. The Greenwater essentially parallels Rd. 70 to the end of the road, but enters a canyon for some of the distance, particularly toward the upper end of the road. The lower end of the Greenwater is accessible on Rd. 7010, which crosses the river off Rd. 70 and immediately runs into a gate. The gate is open to vehicles by permit only. However, when entry is allowed, you can walk down this road and have much of the lower river to yourself on most days when the gate is closed to vehicles. It is 1.4 miles up Rd. 70 to Rd. 7010.

The river contains rainbow, cutthroat, and some brook trout in its upper stretches. While the fish may be smaller farther up the river, it is not as heavily fished and thus more productive, particularly for dry fly fishing.

Selective fishery regulations have helped the Greenwater River. It has a relatively decent population of trout, although of small size,

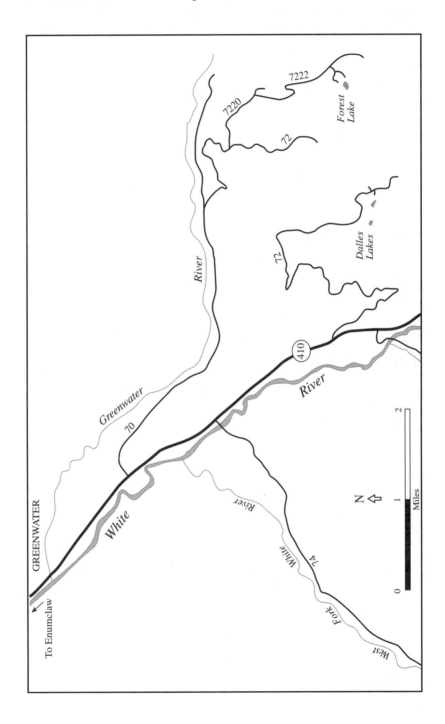

but there are fish in the river to 14 inches in a few spots. It's a very fishable river, with lots of holding water. Fish where no one else does and you will have a pleasant day catching small mountain trout. By midsummer, the river is easily waded, but in some places there is a considerable distance between holding water. Nevertheless, once you're off the beaten path it's worth it to work your way up the river.

Fewer anglers fish the stream beyond the road end, and there are more trout, though they become increasingly smaller. Upstream, the river flows through a variety of areas, becoming pond-like in some places and passes through the Greenwater Lakes and Echo Lake.

Forest Lake.

Forest Lake (3900)

Privately stocked in the past, 2.5 acre Forest Lake is regularly planted by Washington State with rainbow. It occasionally produces a few large rainbow, but has no spawning habitat. It can provide fast action in the early season and would benefit from a 2-fish limit, as it is easily fished. To find it, get a map and have patience: take Rd. 70 from Highway 410, turn onto Rd. 72, then Rd. 7220 to 7222, bear right on a complicated route on a rough road to the lake.

Dalles Lakes (4550)

Dalles Lake No.1 is 2.5 acres and 13 feet deep. Lake No.2 is a 0.8 acre pond. Drive Rd. 70 5.9 miles to Rd. 72. From Rd. 72, continue

6.9 miles to a small spur road that abruptly ends and leads to a 100 foot descent to the first lake. The pond is just a slight cross country effort over the ridge beyond Dalles Lake. Both are rainbow lakes, planted on a 3-year cycle, still somewhat in the process of recovering from devastating old style logging, when every tree was cut right down to the lake's shore. Rainbow grow well in the lakes, a few growing to 16 inches and slightly larger by their fourth year, but they are subject to winterkill. Evidence that fish can live a long time in high lakes is the fact that an 11-year-old cutthroat was caught in Dalles Lake in 1977, 18 inches long.

Greenwater Lakes

Also known as Meeker Lakes, the Greenwater Lakes were named for Ezra Meeker, an early pioneer in Puyallup. The Greenwater River flows in and out of each of them. Lower Greenwater Lake (2780), is 4 acres, and Upper Greenwater (2846), 0.25 miles south of the lower lake, is 6.2 acres. The Greenwater River provides good spawning habitat for the trout in both lakes and they have self-sustaining populations of cutthroat, brook trout and a few rainbow. Both are easily accessible and heavily fished. Drive to the end of Rd. 70. The Greenwater Trail and the Naches Wagon Trail begin here. The Greenwater Trail leads to the lower lake in 1.5 miles, a 200 foot elevation gain, then 0.5 miles further to the upper lake.

Quinn Lake (3380)

A small 1.5 acre lake, Quinn Lake drains through Lost Creek to the Greenwater River, and has some spawning gravel in its inlet. It is 13 feet deep. To reach it, hike 3.25 miles on the Greenwater Trail to Tr. 1185, the Lost Lake trail. After struggling 2.5 rather steep miles up this trail, reach Quinn Lake. It produces eastern brook.

Lost Lake (4000)

Packed with brook trout, 8-9 inches, 26 acre Lost Lake is 0.5 miles beyond Quinn Lake on Tr. 1185.

Echo Lake (3820)

This large, 62 acre, 35 foot deep lake is probably the most thoroughly studied high lake in Pierce County. The lake was formed when a slide dammed the Greenwater River. The river above the lake

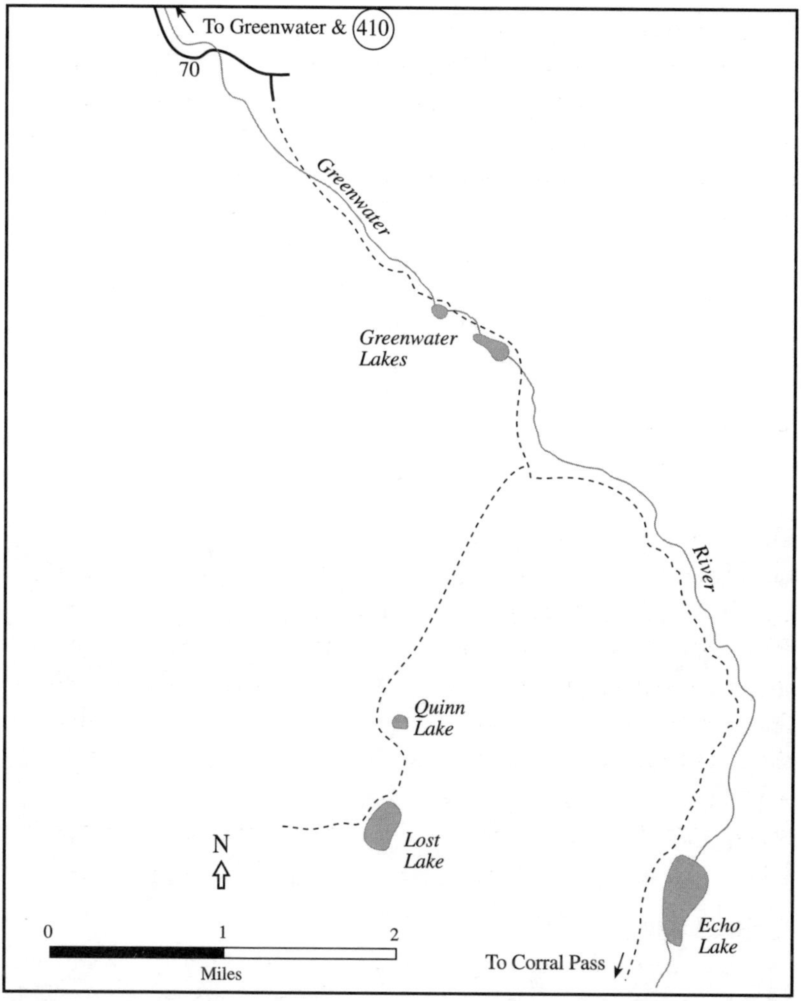

To Greenwater & (410)

70

Greenwater

Greenwater Lakes

River

Quinn Lake

N
⇧

Lost Lake

0   1   2

Miles

To Corral Pass ↓

Echo Lake

provides excellent and almost unlimited spawning habitat to the lake's coastal cutthroat population, probably native to the lake. Despite a healthy population of scuds, the trout are relatively small and thin but very abundant, despite lots of fishing pressure. The average length is about 7-8 inches.

Echo Lake is said to be the most heavily fished high lake in Pierce County, even though it is 7 miles in on the Greenwater Trail, elevation gain 1700 feet, or 6 miles, nearly all downhill, from Corral Pass, a route favored by those who can leave a vehicle at the Greenwater trailhead and arrange transportation to Corral Pass, hiking 13 miles back down to their vehicle.

Huckleberry Creek

The lower stretches of Huckleberry Creek are easily reached from Rd. 73 off Highway 410 and are very heavily fished. If you are going to catch trout in this stream, you have to beat your way through the trees to find a place where no one fishes, because any place that is accessible is pounded. No longer stocked with trout, the creek supports a few rainbow and cutthroat and would probably become a good fishery in the lower stretch with catch and release regulations. There is a trail extending along the upper creek into Mt. Rainier National Park, where the creek is very fast, high gradient and contains small trout.

Mule Lake.

Mule Lake (4600)

An unusual lake with a crater-like depression in the middle, this shallow 2.5 acre lake drains to the West Fork of the White River and supports brook trout, 6-12 inches, with a few lunkers. It is very difficult to fish from shore. Take Rd. 74 from Highway 410 6.4 miles to Rd. 75 for 3.7 miles, then Rd. 7530 to the lake, about 100 feet below the road.

Lonesome Lake (4860)

This 12 acre, 40 foot deep lake is 1 mile past Mule Lake on Rd. 7530. It receives an estimated 3,000 visitors a year, has a fancy bath-

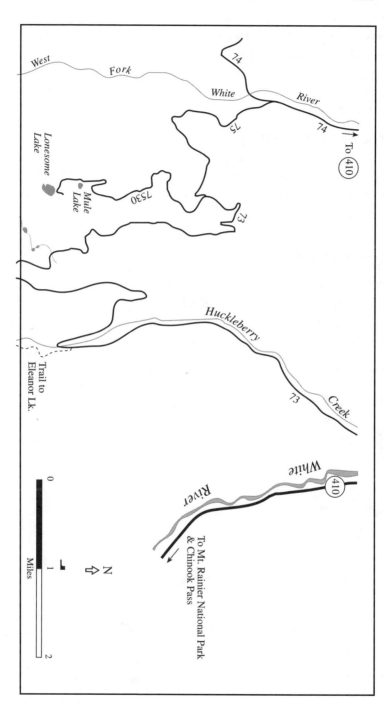

room, and is thus not quite what its name suggests. Despite enormous fishing pressure, it is a testament to the reproductive ability of eastern brook, supporting an overabundant population of brook trout, average size 8 inches, which spawn in its gravelly shoreline. A small lake lies to the southeast cross country, but there are no reports of any fish. Map and compass are required to find it.

Unnamed Lakes (4800)

Southwest of Lonesome Lake, there are three lakes, each about 1 acre in size, draining to a creek which passes under Rd. 73 to Eleanor Creek. All have held trout at one time or another, depending upon stocking practices.

Corral Pass

Rd. 7174 begins 0.4 north of the entrance to Silver Creek Campground, then travels 7 miles to Corral Pass, 5700 feet. From this high elevation pass, several lakes are within reach of the angler willing to hike a bit.

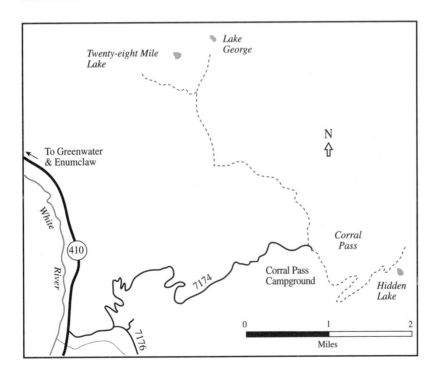

Hidden Lake (4200)

A small 2.5 acre lake, 6 feet deep and generally ice-free by mid-June, its shoreline floods every springtime, producing abundant food for fish. Said to have great potential as a rainbow lake because of an abundant shrimp population, it does not produce great numbers of fish, but there are reports of a few large fish. Rather heavily fished, as it is easily reached by a 2.5 mile trail, Tr. 1176 from Corral Pass.

Twenty-eight Mile Lake (4900)

This very shallow 3 acre lake has no spawning habitat. It was studied in the 1970s and said to have excellent potential but has not been planted for some time. Take the Noble Knob Trail, Tr. 1184 from Corral Pass 3.1 miles to its junction with Dalles Ridge Trail, Tr. 1173, where you find yourself high above Twenty-eight Mile Lake. Continue on Tr. 1173 for about 0.5 miles, then cross country. Map and compass required.

Angler hiking the South Cascades (Chris Axling photo).

Lake George (5470)

Located on the north side of Noble Knob, this 1.5 acre lake is reached by hiking past Twenty-eight Mile Lake on the Noble Knob Trail, then taking Tr. 1184 downhill to the lake, which is off to the right. Cutthroat are planted on a 3-year cycle. Although only 9 feet deep, it is capable of producing good-sized trout. It generally does not become ice-free until mid-July.

Silver Creek/ Crystal Mountain

Silver Creek

The road to Crystal Mountain Resort follows Silver Creek, which runs deep in a canyon much of its length. It runs through a meadow-like flat area as it approaches the resort. The lower stretches are only accessible in a few places along Rd. 174, as private cabins border most of the creek in this area. It contains cutthroat, rainbow and eastern brook but appears to be suffering from nearby development and anglers keeping too many fish in easily accessible spots. The creek would benefit from catch and release regulations and prohibition of bait fishing.

Several lakes are easily accessible in the Crystal Mountain area. Hardy hikers climb the approximately 6 miles from the Crystal Mountain road, on Tr.1163 to where the chairlift drops people off in the summer, at 6776 feet. The lift doesn't begin running in the summer until later in the day than you might hope, so be sure to check on the time. From this point, lakes are found in both directions from the trail. A telephone call to Crystal Mountain Resort is worthwhile to obtain fishing information.

By heading south from the chairlift drop point,walk downhill, through the Miners Lakes, passing to the south of the trail, Elizabeth Lake (5900), 4 acres. Elizabeth has been periodically stocked in times past but has also been reported as barren of trout from time to time. The Miners Lakes, except Upper Henskin and Lower Henskin have been barren of fish periodically and unless containing eastern brook, rely upon stocking to support trout. The Henskin Lakes are most easily reached by a short hike from the Crystal Mountain Resort area. Check with the resort for information.

Upper Henskin Lake (5600)

At 2 acres, the lake contains a population of very small, stunted eastern brook. Lying about 0.25 miles south of the lower lake, it is approximately 10 feet deep.

Lower Henskin Lake (5500)

Much like the upper lake, Lower Henskin produces lots of small brookies.

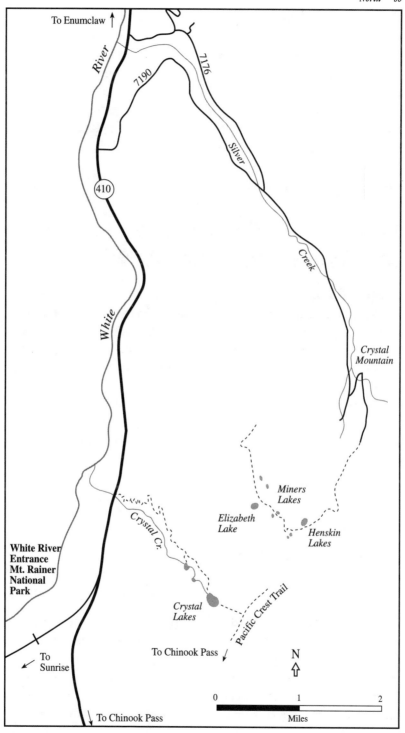

To Enumclaw ↑

River

7190

7176

410

Silver

Creek

White

Crystal Mountain

Crystal Cr.

White River Entrance Mt. Rainer National Park

Miners Lakes

Elizabeth Lake

Henskin Lakes

Crystal Lakes

Pacific Crest Trail

To Chinook Pass ↓

To Sunrise ←

To Chinook Pass ↓

N
⇧

0   1   2

Miles

Crystal Lakes (RNP)

Both Upper Crystal (5830), 9 acres and 40 feet deep, and 12 foot deep, 1.5 acre lower Crystal Lake (5500) are within Mt. Rainier National Park and can be most easily reached by hiking the Pacific Crest trail north from Chinook Pass approximately 3 miles, then dropping down a way trail to the lakes. For those seeking a tougher hike, try the 2.5 mile, 2300 foot elevation gain trail beginning off Highway 410 approximately 4.5 miles inside the Park boundary. Both lakes have historically produced rainbow and cutthroat. Check with the Park for current information.

White River Entrance to Mt. Rainier National Park

Sunrise Point

Shortly after heading toward Sunrise from the White River Entrance, the road crosses Frying Pan Creek. A trail follows the creek for quite a distance. The creek is fast-flowing, glacially colored but extraordinarily scenic. It provides marginal fishing for small trout in its sparse holding water.

A series of lakes are reached by hiking the Palisades Trail from the Sunrise Point parking lot. A day hike will allow you to fish at least one or two lakes without difficulty. There are several lakes without trout along the way.

Sunrise Lake (5800) (RNP)

Visible from the Sunrise Point road, the lake is 25 feet deep, but contains no fish.

Clover Lake (5728) (RNP)

One and a half miles from Sunrise Point trailhead, this beautiful 9 acre relatively deep lake no longer contains trout.

Tom, Dick & Harry Lakes (5700) (RNP)

Two miles from the Sunrise Point trailhead, predominantly downhill and traveling through breathtaking meadows, the trail reaches three shallow lakes. The furthest from the trailhead a small 1.5 acres, Harry Lake, has been subject to a fish removal study by the Park and may not contain trout. Tom and Dick contain no fish.

Hidden Lake (5926) (RNP)

Hidden Lake.

A 20 foot deep, 7 acre lake containing 8-11 inch brook trout, with some lunkers, Hidden Lake is located approximately 900 feet from Harry Lake. After hiking through the meadows along the way to Harry Lake, shortly after passing a rockslide and then a swampy area, follow the steep trail west from the main trail to the lake. If you have made it to the middle of the three lakes, Tom, Dick and Harry, you have gone too far. The way trail continues along the south shore of the lake, then another steep 0.5 miles to an upper basin with a small lake, reported to hold brook trout. Hidden Lake is easy to fish and gives visitors to Mt. Rainier National Park a great combination of a fine hike combined with good fishing.

Green Park Lakes (5400) (RNP)

There are at least three lakes in Green Park. The largest, 12 acre Green Park Lake, is the headwater of Josephine Creek. Naturally reproducing cutthroat trout inhabit it, the descendants of trout first planted more than 75 years ago and last planted in the early 1970s. Averaging 8-10 inches, they have adapted well to their environment. Practice catch and release here or limit your catch to 1 trout a day. Approximately 2 miles northwest of the basin above Hidden Lake, it is a difficult, cross-country hike which crosses a steep scree and talus slope along the way. Map and compass required.

Palisades Lakes (RNP)

A 3.5 mile hike from Sunrise Point allows access to Upper Palisades Lake, (5805) 45 feet deep which contains no fish. The formal trail ends here, but a steep descent of about 500 feet and approxi-

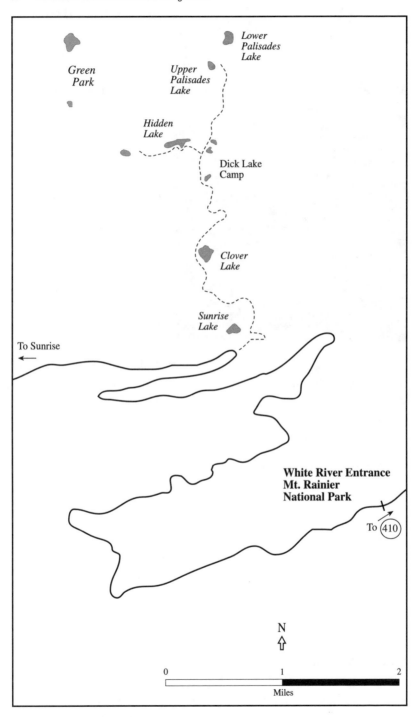

Green
Park

Lower
Palisades
Lake

Upper
Palisades
Lake

Hidden
Lake

Dick Lake
Camp

Clover
Lake

Sunrise
Lake

To Sunrise

White River Entrance
Mt. Rainier
National Park

To (410)

N

0   1   2
Miles

mately 0.5 miles further is 4 acre Lower Palisades Lake (5500). The lake supports brook trout to 14 inches. A 1 acre pond lies 600 feet, west of Lower Palisades Lake in the lake's outlet stream. This pond contains trout, some sizable. Contour map and compass are helpful in finding the lower lake and pond.

Unnamed Lakes (RNP)

There are two unnamed lakes in the area, designated as LW-2 and LW-10 by the Park Service, located in the White River drainage. LW-2 is in the northeast corner of the Park east of Slide Mountain and drains to the White River. It contains cutthroat to 14 inches. LW-10 is west /northwest of Lower Palisades Lake and drains to the creek that feeds Lower Palisades. Few anglers reach either of these lakes, which are both very difficult to find and very brushy. Obtain specific directions from a ranger before attempting to hike to them. Map and compass required.

Sunrise

Forest Lake (5669) (RNP)

Two acres, last reported to have no fish. A slightly complicated route leads from the picnic area at Sunrise approximately 2 miles to Forest Lake. This is a very fine day hike with spectacular scenery, but requires steep downhill hiking on the way in and, of course, steep uphill hiking on the way back.

Unnamed Lake (RNP)

Designated LH-18 by the Park Service, north of Forest Lake, it is found by continuing on the trail past Forest Lake, then cross country to the lake. This lake is approximately 6 acres and contains brook trout, 6-13 inches. Ask a ranger for directions. Map and compass required.

Lake Eleanor (4960) (RNP)

Before the Forest Service constructed Rd. 7350 which branches off Rd. 73 and leading from outside the park to within a moderately easy mile of Eleanor, it took an 8 mile hike from Yakima Park to reach this 20 acre, 40 foot deep lake, one of the largest in the Park. Heavily visited now, it contains naturally reproducing rainbow. Catch and release should be the norm in this lake. Eleanor Creek flows out of the park and down the valley to join Huckleberry Creek. Though the creek holds trout throughout its length, the higher reaches are very difficult to fish.

West

We spent two beautiful days at Mowich. Deer came into the meadow in the evening and trout were leaping for flies that danced over the mirror-like surface of the water.

Floyd Schmoe

Carbon River

Carbon River

Glacially fed, the Carbon River is generally cloudy at best but after a series of cold or freezing nights up on the glacier, it clears some and produces fair to good fishing for small trout, mainly rainbow 6-10 inches. It can be fished early in the season but is better in September and October, after it has dropped to its lowest level and the trout have lined up in the usual feeding lies.

Carbon River.

A dry fly will catch fish, more frequently along the edges, where the water clears a bit, but also in the middle of pools and runs as well when the water clears and the level is low. Dark elkhair caddis or dark mayfly patterns are good performers in September and October. Subsurface fishing works best however, with nymphs and small streamers. The cloudier the water, the deeper you have to fish for success but you will generally have the most success along the edges.

While there are very few large trout in the Carbon River, once it drops into shape it is pleasant to fish. Access is easy along the road when it begins to parallel the river. There is plenty of holding water, lots of riffles and runs. A few miles above Carbonado, the road crosses the river, deep in a canyon below. If you are part mountain goat and want to try water seldom fished, it might be appealing to fish this canyon, as the best fishing in the river seems to be in stair-step boulder and riffle areas. The canyon has that kind of water. Extreme care should be exercised here however. Once in the Park, the road follows the river to the road end and there is plenty of access from the road and the trails which follow the river practically to its source at the Carbon Glacier.

Surprise Lake (4400)

In the days before environmental ethics began to take hold, this 10 acre, fairly shallow lake, was logged to the water's edge. It features a small island. Although rainbow can apparently reproduce at very low rates, it is stocked regularly, as winterkill may occur in severe winters. Depending upon conditions, the lake can be reached by 4-wheel drive or by walking, up an old logging road, left off Carbon River Road, just before reaching Rd. 7810.

Coplay Lake (4100)

Coplay has a good food supply for trout and the 20 acre lake contains eastern brook, 7-9 inches and rainbow. It is 36 feet deep, lies in a large basin and the inlet appears to have spawning potential for lake-dwelling fish. When the roads are in good shape, the lake is easily accessible. Take Rd. 7810 from the Carbon River road for about 1.6 miles, turning right onto Rd. 7820, 0.3 miles to the lake. There is an unnamed lake northwest of Coplay, but there is no information regarding fish. Map and compass are required to find it.

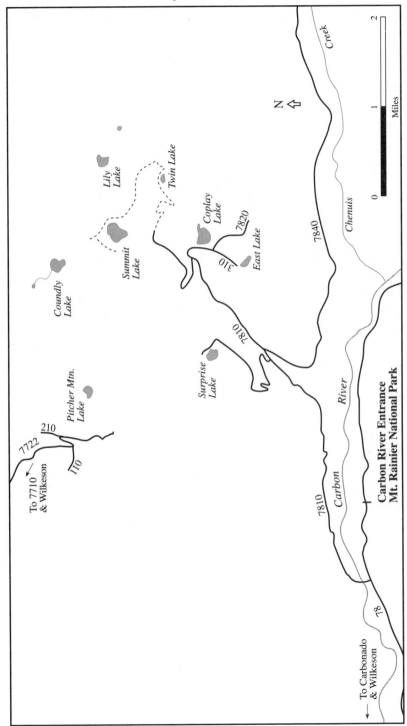

Lily Lake

Twin Lake

Coplay Lake

7820

East Lake

310

Summit Lake

7810

Coundly Lake

Surprise Lake

Pitcher Mtn. Lake

210

7722

To 7710 & Wilkeson

110

Creek

Chenuis

7840

Carbon River

7810

78

Carbon River Entrance
Mt. Rainier National Park

To Carbonado & Wilkeson

N

0   1   2
Miles

East Lake (4000)

Lacking spawning habitat, 4 acre 23 foot deep East Lake is stocked with cutthroat. It is one of the few lakes where biologists found that stocked eastern brook were apparently unable to reproduce successfully. Frequently fished, it is usually ice-free by mid-June. It is reached by continuing straight ahead on Rd. 7810 after it passes Coplay Lake, then 0.5 miles to the lake.

Twin Lake (4800)

An ample number of eastern brook inhabit this 2.5 acre very shallow lake. It is reached by driving to the end of Rd. 7810, rather than taking the turn to Coplay Lake, then by trail 1 mile to the lake, elevation gain 400 feet.

Summit Lake (5440)

One and a half miles north beyond Twin Lake on Tr. 1177, this 25 acre lake slopes steeply to a depth of 190 feet. Grassy open fields with seasonal flowers and a fine view of Mt. Rainier make this a popular destination. It has a large population of eastern brook.

Coundly Lake (4150)

At 16 acres and 85 feet deep, Coundly Lake contains a plentiful supply of eastern brook, some to good size. For those fly fishermen

South Cascades Rainbow.

with a biological bent, one study noted that the larger fish were feeding on large red copepods. The lake is located northwest of Summit Lake and, along with Lily Lake, it can be seen from the top of the ridge on the west side of Summit Lake. It is accessible through a difficult cross country trek. Map and compass work are required.

Lily Lake (4060)

Lily is a rainbow trout lake which can produce fat, sizable fish. The 10 acre, very deep lake lies 0.6 miles cross country from Summit Lake, map and compass required. The outlet stream at the northeast end of the lake, just beyond Lily's small island, drains to Lily Creek and the Clearwater River.

Pitcher Mt Lake (4690)

This 7 acre lake, which has been given a variety of names historically, is 1.6 miles west from Summit Lake, but much more easily reached from Rd. 7722, in turn reached by Rd. 7710 from Wilkeson. There is no established trail to this isolated lake and map and compass are required to find it. It is also known as South Prairie Lake, as it is the headwater of the South Fork of Prairie Creek. A rather shallow lake, it contains rainbow and is planted regularly.

Carbon River Entrance
Mt. Rainier National Park

Three small creeks flow into the Carbon River a few miles inside the Park entrance. All contain small trout. Anglers should use barbless hooks and release all fish, as bull trout inhabit this area and are endangered. Any angler using bait is risking killing an endangered species and terminating trout fishing in these creeks. A number of lakes lying within the Park are accessible by trail or cross country travel from the Carbon River Entrance. Some of these lakes are seldom visited and little is known about whether they contain trout.

Ranger Creek (RNP)

Below Ranger Falls to its confluence with the Carbon River, this creek is fished heavily and contains a few small eastern brook and rainbow.

Chenuis Creek (RNP)

There is very limited fishing below Chenuis Falls for rainbow and eastern brook but a distance above the falls the creek flattens out and there is better fishing for small trout. The upper area is accessible by trail and a Forest Service Road but some serious bushwhacking is necessary.

Ipsut Creek (RNP)

In the approximately 0.5 miles from its mouth on the Carbon River to Ipsut Falls, this creek contains small rainbow and eastern brook.

Green Lake.

Green Lake (2950) (RNP)

The frequently traveled 2 mile trail to Green Lake, 12 acres and 80 feet deep, begins approximately 3.5 miles inside the Carbon River entrance on the right side of the road. The trail gains 1000 feet and is deceptively flat for the first 0.25 miles, then steepens considerably, flattening a bit as it reaches the last stretch to the lake. This is a good trail and good hike for children with some energy. Popular Green Lake yields cutthroat.

Chenuis Lakes (5000) (RNP)

The three Chenuis Lakes are located on Chenuis Mountain, have

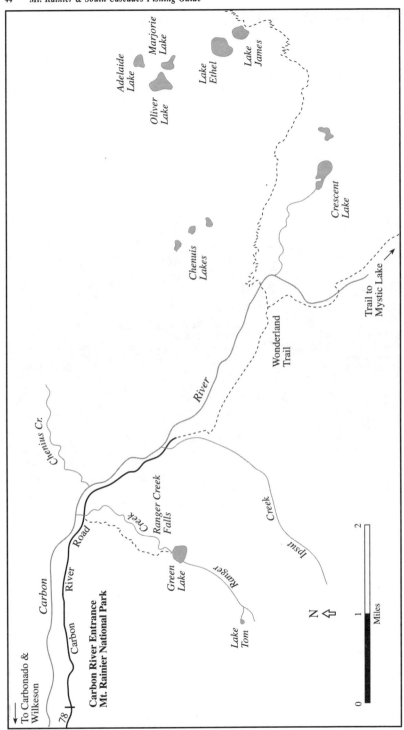

no established trail to them, require cross country hiking and are seldom visited. Of the three, the largest, is approximately 4 acres and nearly 40 feet deep. Contour map and compass are required. Ask a ranger for more specific information. This is a very isolated area of the Park and the trek to the lakes has its rewards simply for that reason. They are believed to contain no trout.

Lake James (4370) (RNP)

A well-known 19 acre, 70 foot deep and very clear lake, James and its fellow first name lakes are a tough but rewarding 8 miles from Ipsut Creek on the Northern Loop Trail. (This route is considerably longer if the Carbon River Road is closed) The lakes may also be reached from outside the Park by taking Rd. 74 from Highway 410 south of Greenwater, to Rd. 7550 up the West Fork White River, hiking about 2 miles up the east side of the river to a junction with the Northern Loop Trail. This road is subject to washouts and may not be open. From the Northern Loop Trail, it is a steep 1200 feet and over another mile to James. There are many lakes in the immediate area but staying with the first name lakes is best for the angler, as all contain Kamloops rainbow.

Lake Ethel.

Lake Ethel (4287) (RNP)

30 acres and over 90 feet deep, 300 feet northwest of James, Ethel is one of the larger lakes in the Park and has long been known for its good rainbow fishing.

Lake Oliver (4558) (RNP)

Accessible by cross country walking from James and Ethel, this very deep 20 acre lake drains to Marjorie Lake.

Lake Marjorie (4555) (RNP)

Marjorie is smaller at 11 acres and shallower than Ethel and Oliver, but it has a self-sustaining population of rainbow trout. It is fed by a creek from Oliver, and is easily accessible from Oliver.

Adelaide Lake (4584) (RNP)

Northeast approximately 0.25 miles from Oliver and Marjorie, 7 acre Adelaide is known for its seasonally warm water and for the legendary report of the netting of a 32 inch rainbow with a set net in 1959.

Mystic Lake (5700) (RNP)

A 6 mile trek from Ipsut Creek gains 3500 feet to reach this 8 acre lake. The hike features a close-up view of Carbon Glacier, plentiful meadows and a side trip to Willis Wall. If you have an aversion to mosquitos, avoid this lake until August. It produces cutthroat.

Mowich Lake Entrance
Mt. Rainier National Park

Evans Creek

This creek holds small trout but is extremely difficult to fish because it is so brushy. It can be reached off the Mowich road at Evans Creek Campground and above and below that point.

Upper Mowich River (RNP)

The seldom fished upper Mowich can be reached by hiking 3.5 miles from Mowich Lake, gradually downhill at first but dropping about 1600 feet in less than 2 miles at the end, which must inevitably be followed by the steep uphill hike to get back. Few anglers are willing to make the trip. The river is often discolored during the sum-

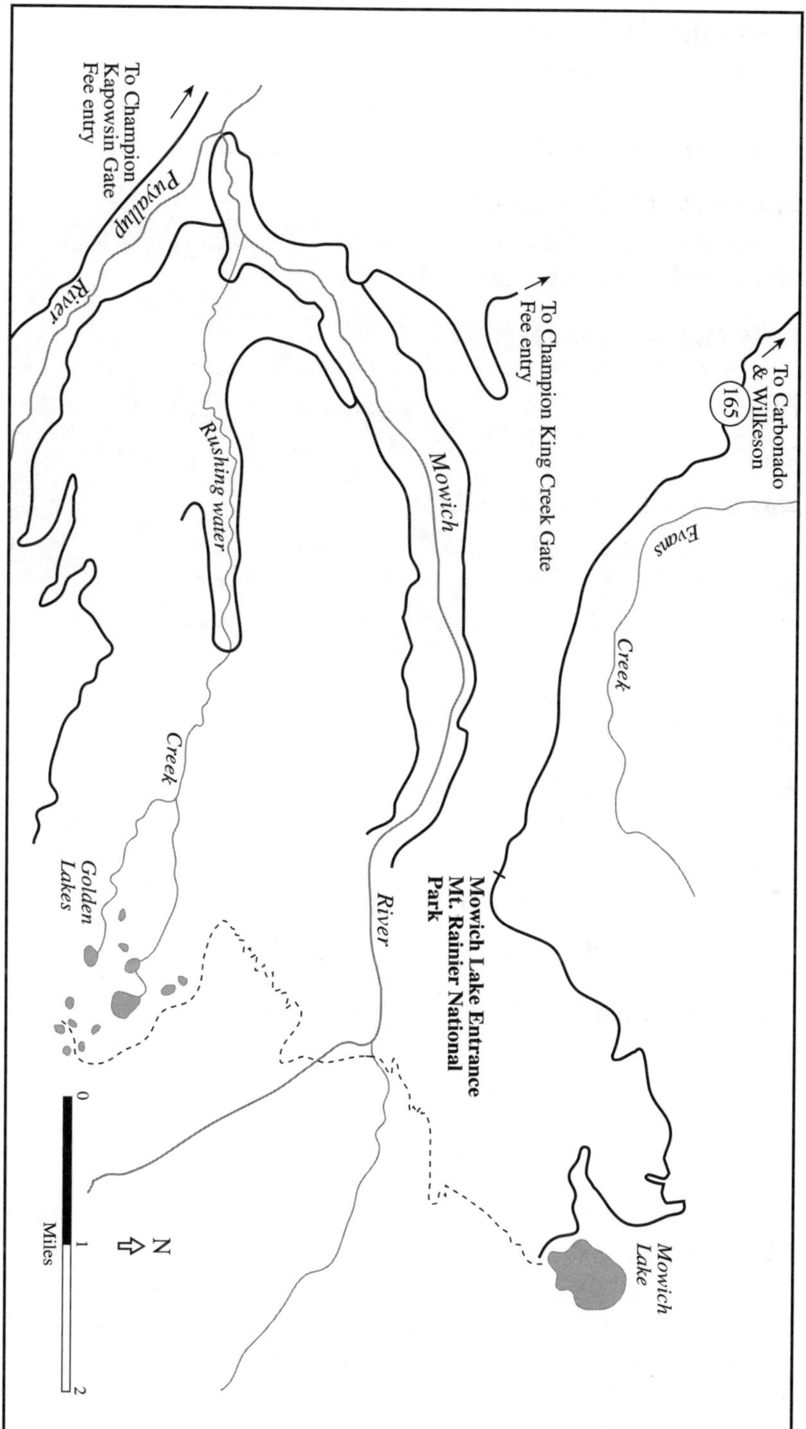

To Champion
Kapowsin Gate
Fee entry

Puyallup

River

To Champion King Creek Gate
Fee entry

165

To Carbonado
& Wilkeson

Rushing water

Mowich

Evans

Creek

Creek

Golden
Lakes

Mowich Lake Entrance
Mt. Rainier National
Park

River

Mowich
Lake

0   1   2

Miles

N

mer and is subject to substantial fluctuations in size due to glacial melt and rainfall. When clear early and late in the season, it can be fished successfully for cutthroat and rainbow.

Mowich Lake.

Mowich Lake (4929) (RNP)

At 100 acres and 190 feet deep, Mowich is the largest lake in the Park. It is located at the end of Mowich Road, with limited camping. The lake contains kokanee and there are reports of eastern brook. It has a number of spots along its shoreline where it can be fished. Be sure to obey all barriers and signs restricting access to the shoreline—too much damage to the shoreline could result in a total restriction of fishing to protect this alpine environment. It is best fished from a float tube or rubber raft.

Crater Creek (RNP)

For those anglers dying to bushwhack, Crater Creek produces small eastern brook. The creek drains out of Mowich Lake and downhill steeply, but does flatten out a bit and pools can be fished after a serious thrash through the woods. Trout apparently swim out of Mowich Lake and down this creek, inhabiting the few pools available to them.

Golden Lakes (RNP)

Located in Sunset Park, the Golden Lakes comprise a group of lakes and small ponds. The largest Golden Lake (4556) is 18 acres, 20 feet deep; another 9 acre lake (4450) at one time held Loch Leven trout; a third (4950) is 4 acres. The largest lake contains brook trout and there are reports of brook and cutthroat being caught in all three lakes and in some other lakes and ponds in the vicinity. Since there are more than 10 lakes here, a bit of exploring is worthwhile for the angler. Accessible by trail from the Westside Road when open, it is more easily reached by driving 0.5 miles from the Mowich Lake entrance to the Paul Peak picnic area where the trail leads 3.5 miles with a steep descent to the Wonderland Trail. Turn right and hike another 4 miles, steeply at the end, to the Golden Lakes. The lakes are also reached from Champion Co. property roads but the road system is complicated, the trail is not maintained, sometimes there are gate closures and an overnight fee has been charged for staying at the lakes.

Champion Company Land

Champion Pacific Timberlands Inc. is the owner of a very large tract of land which borders on Carbonado to the north, Kapowsin to the west, Ashford to the south and Mt. Rainer National Park on the east. Entry is by fee permit only, which may be obtained at stores in the Kapowsin area. There are two entry gates, Kings Creek Gate north of Lake Kapowsin and Kapowsin Gate. While the entry fee is a deterrent to anglers, it is worth it to many and affords the opportunity to travel about and fish a large area without much company. Be sure to obtain a map and information, as the road system is very complex.

Lake Kapowsin (600)

Located just outside the entrance to Champion Co. land, Kapowsin is 512 acres, a weedy natural lake open to the public and popular with fly anglers.

Puyallup and Mowich Rivers

Long stretches of the upper Puyallup river and much of the Mowich River are available to anglers. Both rivers, small to medium size, are clouded by the glaciers from which they originate, and are generally opaque most of the season, with some clearing resulting after a series of very cold nights.

Some locals claim there is very good fishing in both rivers but others find it a tough day's outing on either. Subsurface fishing is

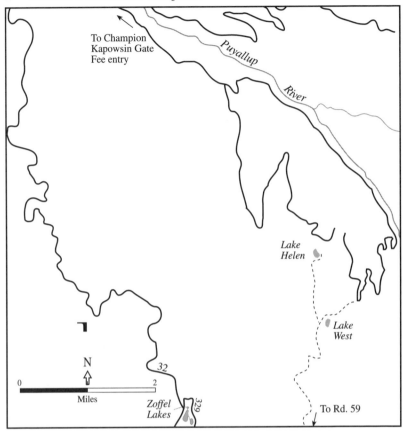

generally necessary but clearing conditions can result in some success on dry flies. The Mowich is generally much less turbid than the
Puyallup, which most of the time is too muddy to fish.

Since both the upper Puyallup and the Mowich rivers have long
been above the range of anadromous fish due to a dam on the Puyallup
River, the resident trout have had the streams to themselves. However,
this could all change, as there are plans to enable anadromous fish to
pass beyond these dams. Getting to know these two rivers has been
worth the effort for some anglers, who swear by the results.

Voight Creek

A clear flowing creek north of the Puyallup river, Voight Creek
runs for several miles and contains fair numbers of small trout.

Neisson Creek

This creek flows into the Puyallup just below the confluence of the

Mowich and the Puyallup. It is crossed by roads traveling upstream and provides fair to good fishing for small trout, primarily cutthroat.

Rushing Water Creek

Accessible by a road which parallels the south side of the Mowich River, this clear flowing creek affords good fishing for cutthroat and cuttbows. It travels through some beaver pond areas worth exploring by anglers.

Upper Mashel River

The small Mashel River's upper forks are both on Champion Land and are rarely fished. Both have small trout in good numbers.

Lake Mary Lea

Lying west of the Upper Mashel River, it is unknown whether this lake and the pond to its north contain trout. If not, Mary Lea would be a good candidate for stocking.

Zoffel Lakes (4400)

Also known as Paul Bunyan Lakes, these three small lakes, the largest of which is 6 acres, drain to Busy Wild Creek. They produce cutthroat. At the very edge of Champion property but only accessible through the Champion gates, these three high mountain lakes are seldom visited and fished.

Nisqually River

Highway 706 from Elbe to the Nisqually Entrance of Mt. Rainier National Park affords anglers access to several lakes and to the Nisqually River.

Anderson Lakes (3920)

Along with Lower Anderson, 8 acre, 39 foot deep Upper Anderson drains to Lake Creek then to the Nisqually River. Though at times when road conditions allow, easily reached and frequently fished, both Anderson Lakes have an over-abundant population of stunted brook trout. Both are good places to fish with small children, keeping a limit of brook trout, which range to 8-9 inches. The lakes are accessible through a complicated maze of roads beginning at National or Ashford, heading south, off Rd. 100, or from Big Creek Campground through yet another complicated maze of logging roads off Rd. 85.

Pothole, Bertha May and Granite Lakes

The trailhead to these lakes is found by driving south on Rd. 52 approximately 10 miles from Elbe, crossing the Nisqually, turning left, traveling past Big Creek Campground, then right on Rd. 84, and right again on Rd. 8410, following it to the trailhead of Tr. 251. All of these lakes have lots of visitors but are quite difficult to fish from shore due to heavy shoreline vegetation. A float tube, raft or chest waders are most helpful, particularly for fly anglers.

Pothole Lake (3700)

An easy 0.8 miles from the trailhead, 6 acre Pothole is a steady producer of cutthroat. The area surrounding the lake is endowed with some of the finest blueberry bushes found in the northwest.

Bertha May Lake.

Bertha May Lake (4055)

A short but quite steep .8 miles beyond Pothole by trail, Bertha May is 30 acres and a very deep 110 feet. Spring fed, it has a large population of sculpin and is regularly stocked. A muddler minnow might bring a large rainbow. The lake is extremely difficult to fish from shore.

Granite Lake (4163)

Twenty-nine acres, this rather deep lake is supplied primarily by

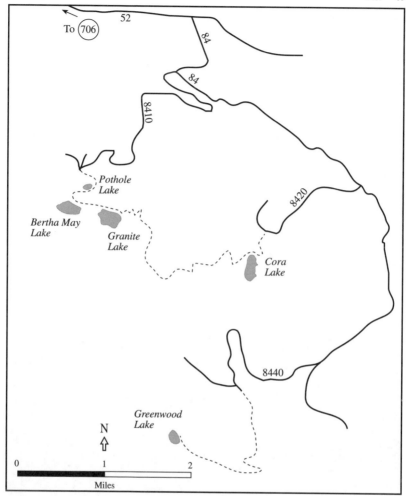

springs and has only marginal spawning habitat. Nevertheless, the
lake contains abundant brook trout to 8-9 inches. As the trail passes
just above it, there is a grand view of Mt. Rainier. It is 0.5 miles on
the trail beyond Bertha May Lake. There is great mushroom picking
near the lake in the fall for those who know their mushrooms.

Cora Lake (3900)

To fish Cora Lake, follow the directions to Pothole Lake, but in-
stead of turning off Rd. 84 onto Rd. 8410, continue on to Rd. 8420,
turn right and follow it to a trail leading left uphill off the road a steep
800 feet in 0.8 miles to the lake. The trail passes two unique water-
falls where water fans out over terraced bedrock. The lake is 28 acres,

and 57 feet deep. It is popular due to its close proximity to the road, but that nearly 1 mile hike is steep. The lake supports stocked rainbow and has historically also held eastern brook.

Greenwood Lake (4450)

Long a producer of a self-sustaining population of chunky eastern brook trout to 10 inches and larger, Greenwood Lake is 7 acres and 30 feet deep. To find it, follow the directions to Cora Lake, following Rd. 84 past the turnoff to Cora, continuing on the right on Rd. 8440 until the road crosses the trailhead for High Rock and Greenwood Lake Tr. 253, The lake is a pleasant 3 mile hike. A shorter route can be taken off Rd. 85, to Rd. 8511, then to Tr. 253.

Copper Creek

Just 3.8 miles toward Mt. Rainier National Park from Ashford, Rd. 59, the Copper Creek Road, leads north to several lakes, accessible by trail.

Lake Christine.

Lake Christine (4700)

Christine is 4.5 acres, 14 feet deep, and surrounded by meadow. Particular care should be exercised in fishing it, as the shoreline has been heavily impacted by use. The lake has historically held cutthroat, rainbow, and brook trout and has good spawning gravel in its inlet. The cutthroat and rainbow may no longer be present in this lake. Drive Rd. 5920 from Rd. 59 then take Tr. 249, about 1 mile, quite steep in places, to the lake.

Beljica Ponds (4500)

This shallow series of small ponds can be reached by either hiking beyond Lake Christine another mile on Tr. 249, or by driving Rd. 59 to its junction with the trailhead to Goat Lake, Tr. 248, then hiking a flat 0.5 miles to Beljica Meadows and the ponds, which contain cutthroat.

Goat Lake (4300)

A scenic 10 acre lake, which drains to Goat Creek, it is 25 feet deep, has a good spawning area in the outlet, and supports a population of fat eastern brook ranging from 8 to 13 inches. To reach the lake, follow the directions to Beljica Ponds, continue north, then west on Tr. 248 1.5 miles to the lake.

Lake West.

Lake West (4600)

Also known as Hidden Lake, along with countless other lakes, this is a productive 6 acre lake known for fat, healthy rainbow trout. Take Rd. 59 to Tr. 267 and hike 2.5 miles, then 0.5 miles on a spur trail east to Lake West, gaining about 600 feet, then descending sharply 600 feet to the lake.

Lake Helen (4000)

Periodically planted with rainbow, some natural reproduction apparently also takes place in this 5 acre lake, although the trout are unsuccessful in spawning in some years. Lake Helen is 17 feet deep and has historically produced good-sized trout. At one time it was planted with Montana Black-Spot, some of which apparently survived, perhaps along with other planted cutthroat. The trout spawn in the outlet stream, which should be treated very carefully. There is a fisherman's trail around the lake, but because it is located in a steeply-sloped basin, fishing from the shoreline is difficult. Helen is located 1.3 miles beyond the spur trail to Lake West. There is also road access from Champion Co. property to within about 0.5 miles of the lake. Catch and release is an appropriate practice here.

Nisqually Entrance Mt. Rainier National Park

Nisqually River (RNP)

A medium size glacially colored river, the Nisqually is nearly always opaque and brown in color, but contains trout from at least Longmire downstream. Not worth the effort to fish with a dry fly, it can be fished using wet flies, nymphs and streamers. Spin fishermen generally are more successful in this river, except on those rare occasions when the river clears enough to allow decent fly fishing. When the Nisqually is running brown and high, try fishing another water. October is the best month to fish the river, which contains surprising numbers of rainbow and cutthroat.

Tahoma Creek (RNP)

Very much discolored from the first warm weather until freezing nights are consistent, the creek does contain fair numbers of trout. It is simply not worth fishing when it is not clear, which is most of the time.

Fish Creek (RNP)

Accessible above its junction with Tahoma Creek, about 2 miles up the Westside Road above the site of the road washout, Fish Creek

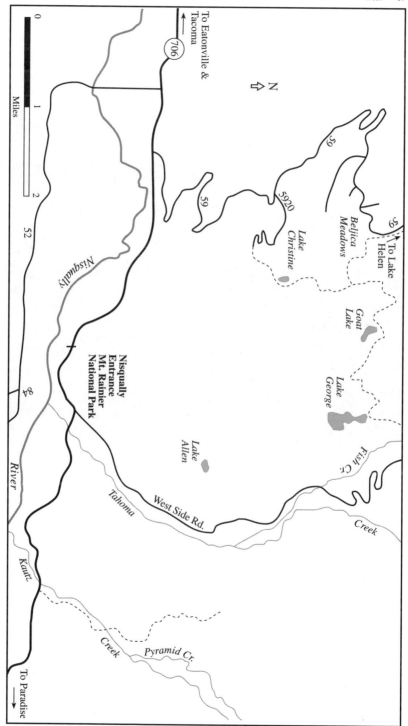

is a very small clear-flowing creek, with holes spaced quite a distance apart. In the past a fine little creek to fish, the streambed has been heavily affected by natural flood runoff. Lots of blowdown makes for hard going, clambering over enormous fallen trees to reach the next hole. Fishable without waders because it is so small, it contains a few small cutthroat, to 9 inches. As its flow diminishes during the summer, trout will drop down into Tahoma Creek. There are very few fish in this creek and catch and release is imperative.

Lake George.

Lake George (4232) (RNP)

When the Westside Road is open, this 33 acre lake is very popular. It is well-known for its abundant sculpin, i.e., bullhead, which no doubt were brought to the lake long ago to be used as bait, but also holds plenty of brook trout, some of which are reported to reach large size. Easily reached by a flat 1 mile trail when the Westside Road is open, it is a much longer trek when the road is closed. A mountain bike trip to the trailhead and a walk to the lake becomes a good day trip when the road is closed.

Lake Allen (RNP)

This 5 acre lake once held large rainbow and cutthroat. A very difficult cross country hike, extremely steep, map and compass required, mountaineering skills needed, it has been reported to be barren of fish.

Kautz Creek (RNP)

Often clear flowing, particularly early and late in the season, Kautz is a sizable creek with enough holding water to make flyfishing interesting and enjoyable. It is crossed by the main road approximately 3 miles inside the park from the Nisqually Entrance and readily fishable both downstream to its junction with the Nisqually and upstream for at least a couple of miles. A trail follows it upstream and then crosses it in 1.5 miles.

The creek flows through a washed out valley which is subjected to vast fluctuations in the creek due to seasonal changes and runoff. Kautz Creek was the site of an enormous mudflow in 1947, when a flood estimated to carry over 50 million cubic yards of rocks, soil, trees, and every other imaginable kind of debris charged down through the site of the present creek. The immensity of the mudflow can be visualized by considering that the site of the Nisqually Road over Kautz Creek is built on top of the mudflow. The creek has been meandering through it ever since and it is not a scenic creek but carries trout to 10 inches and slightly larger. Its trout population is fragile and as with all streams in the Park, barbless hooks and catch and release are in order.

Pyramid Creek (RNP)

A small creek which feeds Kautz Creek above the point where the trail crosses Kautz, it contains small rainbow and cutthroat.

Paradise

Paradise River (RNP)

The Paradise river is appropriately named. A very beautiful, small river, it is clear flowing and fishable early in the season. It joins the Nisqually River across from Cougar Flats Campground. A short walk from the road, crossing the Nisqually, takes you to it. Although lovely and containing trout, the Paradise River is very difficult to fish due to its lack of holding water and brushy, tree lined banks. Thrashing through bushes and trees precedes all successful angling on this river. The trail upriver to Narada Falls provides access continuing upstream until the gradient is too high for any holding water. Short casting, mainly dapping a dry fly or nymph into holding spots with ultralight gear, provides a few hours of enjoyable fishing and considerable exer-

Paradise River.

cise on the Paradise River. There are not a lot of trout in the river and catch and release should always be the rule.

Above Narada Falls, particularly in the Paradise Valley, the river runs through a spectacular area, has more holding water, but appears not to contain trout. The falls historically blocked migration upstream, and there are no records of this stretch of river ever being stocked.

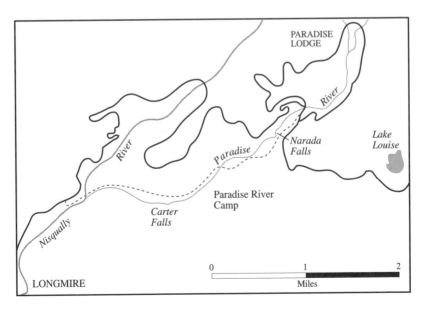

Stevens Creek (RNP)

Stevens Creek is a large, almost river size creek, clear except during periods of heavy runoff. From its headwaters, it rushes through Stevens Canyon, far below the road, for about 3 miles to its junction with the Muddy Fork of the Cowlitz. It contains eastern brook, rainbow and cutthroat. The easiest access is from Box Canyon Parking Lot downhill about 0.7 miles to the Wonderland Trail, then either upstream or downstream. The Wonderland Trail roughly follows the creek upstream and crosses it in approximately 1.5 miles.

Stevens Creek.

A beautiful stream with some very deep holes, it is mostly pocket water. It is easier to wade at low water, but wading anytime is hard work, requiring the angler to get out of the creek and bushwhack along the banks and through the woods to find good spots. Early in the season, expect to find trout in the deep holes and unwilling to rise to flies. During this time, it is easy to get the impression that there are no fish in the creek. They don't seem to feed avidly until later (or until the angler improves his or her technique) and even then, alas, they rarely rise readily to a dry fly, leading one to the conclusion that surface feeding is infrequent in Stevens Creek. The difficulty in persuading trout to your fly here is substantially alleviated by the stunning color and beauty of the creek. Plunking weighted nymphs into

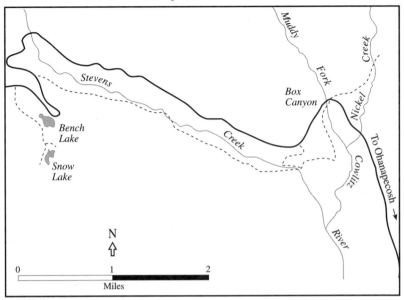

the holes is most effective at this time. Dry fly fishing is more productive later in the season as the water level drops and the fish
spread out into pockets and feeding stations.

Reflection Lakes (RNP)

The Park Service attempted to remove all brook trout living in
Reflection Lake. On a summer night, at dusk, stop at the lake to see
the results—many bulging rises all over the lake. Brook trout inhabit
both lakes and the wetlands and streams flowing through them behind the lakes. **There is no fishing**, necessitated by the heavy use of
the shoreline, its degradation and the need to preserve it.

Louise Lake (4592) (RNP)

Sixty feet deep, 17 acres and adjacent to the Paradise-Ohanepacosh
road, just east of Reflection Lakes, Louise has a rough trail around parts
of it. There are also inlet creeks not far off the trail, where trout like to
gather. It contains an overabundant population of small brook trout.
Catch and release is pointless in this lake, as the size of Louise's trout
would only benefit from anglers catching and keeping the legal limit.
Long ago, before it became so overpopulated, there were reports of
lunker brookies to 4 lbs. More recently, brook trout were 10-12 inches
in this lake but as fishing decreased and harvest was reduced, the lake
gradually became overpopulated and the average size diminished.

Bench Lake (4600) (RNP)

Heavily visited, only a 0.5 mile scenic walk off the Paradise-Ohanepacosh road, Bench Lake contains a healthy number of eastern brook. Anglers might consider bringing a float tube, as fishing from shore is difficult and some very large brookies have been taken here early in the morning and near dark. If you are going to stay for the late bite, be sure to leave before it gets dark and bring a flashlight along, as the going can be difficult on the way in the dark.

Snow Lake (4678) (RNP)

By hiking 0.75 miles uphill by trail beyond Bench Lake, anglers fish this deep lake lying below Unicorn Peak and fed by Unicorn Creek. It contains brook trout and cutthroat and there have been some reports of rainbow. The lake has some limited successful spawning, which accounts for the cutthroat and rainbow. The brookies are good size and predacious.

Nickel Creek (RNP)

Hike the steep, 1 mile trail from Box Canyon, 10 miles from the Stevens Canyon Entrance, to Nickel Creek. Cross the creek and continue up the trail through the woods approximately 0.25 to 0.5 miles, drop down to the creek, and begin fishing. This very small stream has a surprising quantity of chunky 6-9 inch cutthroat, cutbow and rainbow. It is clear-flowing and can be fished earlier than many of the streams in the Park. Barbless hooks and catch and release should be the rule here, because this is a healthy population of mountain trout, well in balance with its stream and food supply.

South

The forests. . . are the most magnificent on the continent. On account of the dense forests, the scenery throughout the region is wild and picturesque. At a few localities glimpses were obtained of the great snow-clad dome of Mount Rainier, rising far over the intervening tree-covered areas.

I.C. Russell

Randle

Silver Creek

Silver Creek flows right through the town of Randle. Take Kindle Road off Highway 12 to Silver Brook Road, turning right, crossing the creek, then turning left on Rd. 47 to head upstream. At the bridge, one can park and hike up the fisherman's trail on the left side of the river and begin fishing. There is a long stretch of creek upstream from here and plenty of small fish. A 12 incher is a lunker in the lower creek.

Silver Creek cutthroat.

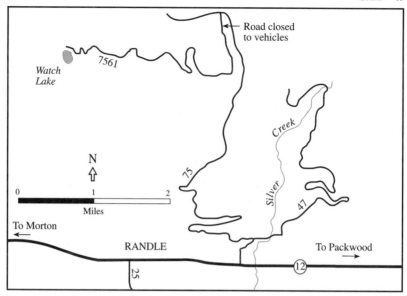

Rd. 47 provides access to the upper stretches of Silver Creek, roughly paralleling the creek, high above it. There are a couple of side roads that come closer, but the creek flows far below in a canyon, very difficult to reach. Exercise caution in trying to reach it, as the Forest Service has on occasion had to rescue persons who were able to get in but could not get out. It is 9.2 miles to Road 85 which crosses Silver Creek. At this point, the creek is fairly small but holds cutthroat, rainbow and cuttbows, the largest probably 10-11 inches. It is heavily fished from this bridge and one must work upstream or downstream. There is good holding water, in some places waist deep.

Silver Creek is a no bait, selective fishery and the results are beginning to show as fishing here is much better than it was before the imposition of these regulations.

Watch Lake (3600)

Fifteen acres and 55 feet deep, Watch Lake is accessible up a complicated road route beginning across from the Randle District Ranger Station. Drive Rd. 75, then left to Rd. 7561 which is washed out and likely to stay that way. Walk from here. It appears that there is some natural reproduction by cutthroat in this lake, it is stocked regularly, and has a reputation for producing large fish at times.

Cispus River

The mainstem Cispus River is quite large and significantly affected by glacial melt downstream from its junction with Muddy Fork Creek, which originates on the slopes of Mount Adams. Above this point, it is clear and fishable for small eastern brook and other species. Below the junction with the Muddy Fork, the Cispus is an early and late season stream, with late season best, after the glacial melt and runoff have fully subsided, generally by mid-September.

This river is well worth exploring and is rumored to hold some sizable trout. Very much a hit and miss river, at times fishing can be excellent and on other occasions, you might believe that there are no fish in the river. It contains rainbow, cutthroat, eastern brook and whitefish. Rd. 23 also known as the Cispus River Road, leads to the mainstem Cispus River and the North Fork.

Lone Tree Lake (3880)

A shallow, mud bottomed 2.5 acre lake, Lone Tree can produce cutthroat 12-15 inches. It is regularly planted. The ice usually comes off it early in May. Drive Rd. 23 6.5 miles to Rd. 55, take the first left uphill, Rd. 012. This road is often washed out but if walking is

necessary, it is only about 1 mile to the lake. Stay straight on the road, do not take the forks to the left. Eventually the road curves to the right at its end. The lake is situated off to the right.

Yellowjacket Creek

Take Rd. 28 off Rd. 23 for approximately 1 mile, to reach a bridge crossing Yellowjacket Creek. Rd. 28 parallels the creek, which runs deep in a canyon much of the way. Mountain goat type fishermen report

Yellowjacket Creek.

good success here. It is a clear-flowing stream, fishable early in the season and has selective fishery regulations. Rainbow predominate, with some cutthroat.

North Fork Cispus River

The North Fork Cispus is a clear-running, beautiful river. It is first accessible from the North Fork Campground, adjacent to Rd. 23. Hike up the trail across the foot bridge and fish nearly as far as you like upstream. This section of the river features small rainbow, with a few larger ones exceeding 10 inches. Rd. 22 splits off north from Rd. 23 and heads up the North Fork. Rd. 2203 forks off to the north just past Swede Creek and follows the river for a few miles, but access to the river is generally better by staying on Rd. 22. Farther upstream, cutthroat comprise more of the trout population. The river also contains whitefish.

Blue Lake (4058)

This very large, 127 acre lake, is also very deep. Small brookies dominate the lake but there is some natural reproduction by cutthroat and rainbow, thought to occur in both inlets, so stay out of them and do not disturb this pristine spawning habitat. The lake is popular but can handle quite a bit of fishing pressure. A float tube or raft is useful. Practice catch and release with rainbow and cutthroat in this fine lake. To fish it, drive Rd. 23 up the Cispus River to Blue Lake Trail, hike approximately 3.8 miles to the lake, an elevation gain of about 2000 feet.

Bishop Ridge Lakes (4240)

Several lakes, some of which are unnamed, are located in the Bishop Ridge Area. Bishop Ridge Lake, a small, 2.5 acre lake, is accessible by driving Rd. 22 to Rd. 78, turning south, then onto Rd. 7802, which passes within a few hundred feet of the lake. It drains to the North Fork Cispus River. There is a small lake lying to the south of Bishop Ridge Lake, sometimes called Upper Bishop, reached by traveling Rd. 7802, just past Bishop Ridge Lake, to the end of spur Rd. 669, then cross country approximately 0.3 miles. Map and compass are required. Both lakes have historically been stocked.

Mud Lake (4864)

A very shallow 7.5 acres, this lake is aptly named, but relatively productive, and anglers can catch cutthroat to 12 inches. Follow the

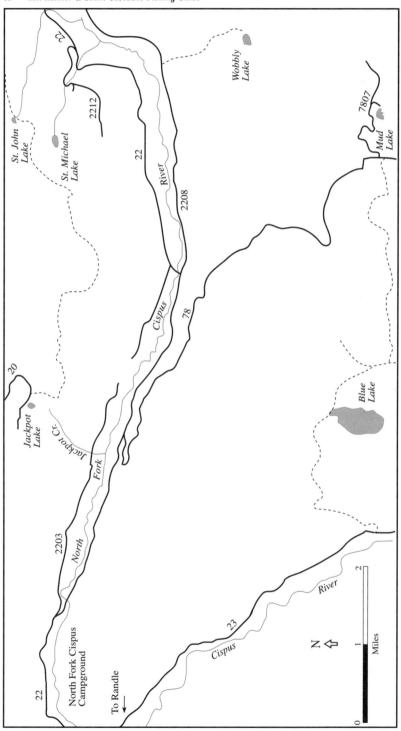

directions to Bishop Ridge Lake, continue on Rd. 78 to Rd. 7807, and eventually pass the lake just before the Hamilton Butte trailhead, by turning on spur 027 to the lake.

Wobbly Lake.

Wobbly Lake (3300)

Varying in size from about 10 acres to 1 acre, depending upon the time of year, this lake has the distinction of producing a 9 pound state record brook trout in 1988. However, it generally contains a very abundant population of 7-11inch brook trout. The 9 pound brookie was caught eight years after an attempt was made to "rehabilitate" the lake and its inlet with rotenone, and is considered a fluke occurrence. The effort also demonstrated that it is nearly impossible for human beings to completely eliminate brook trout from mountain lakes. Only winterkill apparently eliminates the hardy brook trout. It is reached by continuing on Rd. 22 past Rd. 78, then taking Rd. 2208 to the trailhead which begins just before Wobbly Creek. Hike from this point 1.8 miles to the lake.

St. Michael Lake (4750)

Rainbow are able to reproduce in limited numbers in the outlet of this 9 acre, 30 foot deep lake and great care should be exercised in this stream area. The rainbow can reach good size but are few in number and are supplemented by periodic cutthroat plants. Catch and release for rainbow should be the norm in this lake. Access is by trail or bushwhack up St. Michael Creek. Stay on the right-hand side of the creek or you will end up in some rock cliffs that make access to the lake very difficult and dangerous. Follow Rd. 22 past Rd. 2208 then left on Rd. 2212 to its junction with Rd. 025. Walk from here. Map and compass are required.

St. John Lake (5100)

St. John is a 3 acre, very beautiful tear drop shape lake. Fish cannot reproduce in the lake and stocking is necessary to maintain a population of trout. Check with the State to see if it has been stocked. It lies adjacent to Tr. 7, which begins at Jackpot Lake. It is also reached by hiking the same trail from its east end near Hugo Lake.

Packwood

Cowlitz River

Old-timers and experts know where and how to fish the Cowlitz. There are large rainbow and cutthroat in this river along with lots of whitefish. There are also enticing rumors about brown trout. However, the lunkers are generally found in very deep holes, which are difficult to fish, particularly when fly fishing. Below the confluence with the Muddy Fork, from July on, the Cowlitz is heavily silted and not really fishable. Above this point, it is clear-flowing but expertise is needed to lure its large fish out of hiding.

Hall Creek

Highway 12 crosses Hall Creek just west of Packwood. This unusual creek has spring creek like characteristics at its lower end as it flows into a large oxbow and Johnson Creek. It has brown trout, the origin of which is somewhat mysterious. Access is difficult, and exploring may be worthwhile here. It is very slow-moving but does have riffles and holes. Hall Creek also contains rainbow and cutthroat. Private property borders much of the creek, and the owners' rights must be respected. Given enough time and energy, some may find this creek to be worth the effort.

Jackpot Lake (4551)

A very popular 5 acre lake, quite shallow and subject to winterkill, Jackpot is regularly stocked with cutthroat, which can grow to good size. It is reached by a long drive up Rd. 20 heading south off Highway 12 just before it crosses Smith Creek.

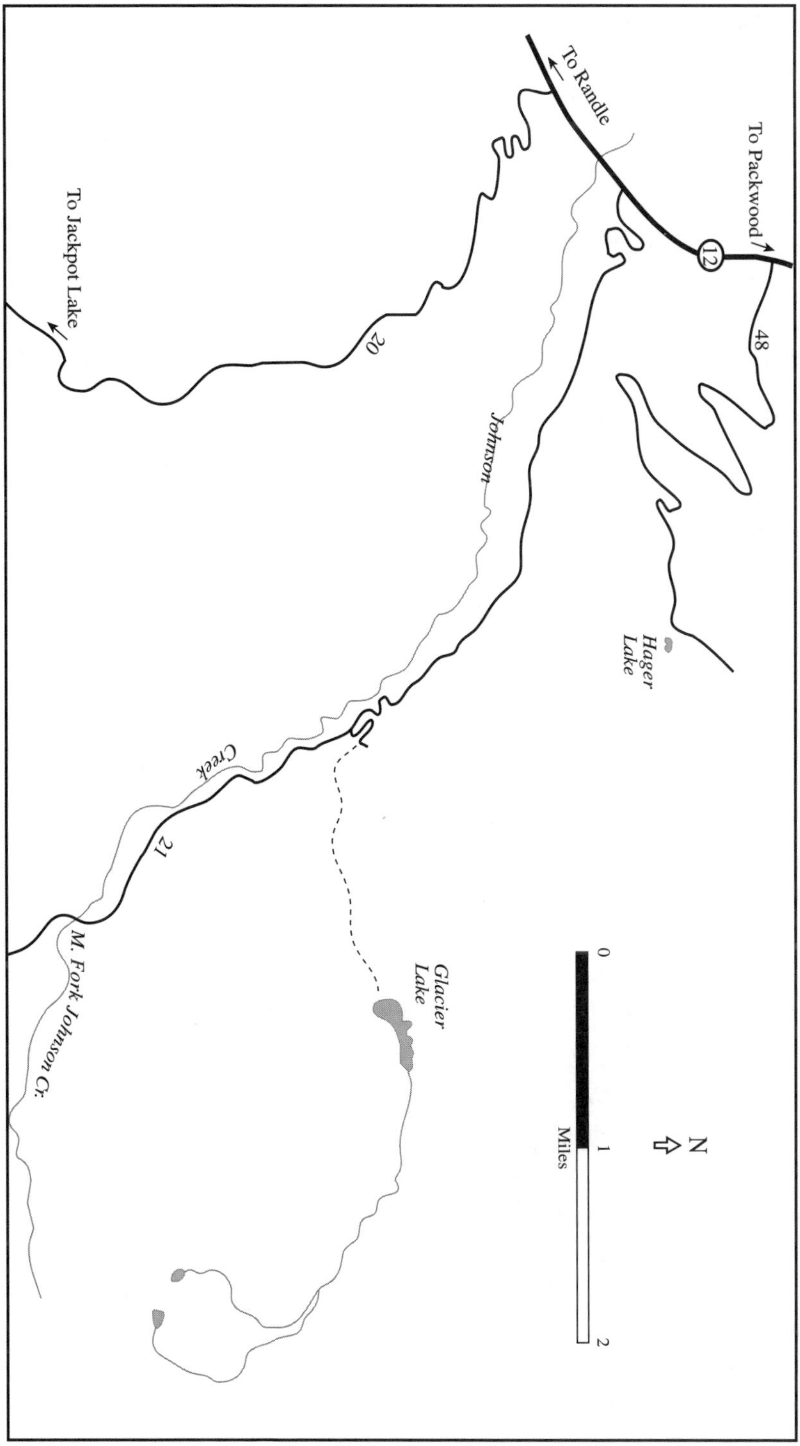

To Randle

To Packwood

To Jackpot Lake

12

48

20

Johnson

Creek

12

M. Fork Johnson Cr.

Hager Lake

Glacier Lake

N

Miles

0 1 2

Hager Lake (2880)

Take Rd. 48 east from Highway 12, approximately 1 mile south of Packwood, then left on Rd. 4830 0.1 miles to the lake, which is essentially a wide spot in Hager Creek with considerable spawning habitat available. A float tube or boat is necessary to catch fish. This lake has historically been a brook trout lake, containing lots of healthy brookies to 6-12 inches and fun to catch. It has periodically been planted with cutthroat, but they have not met with much success. Hager is fishable on opening day due to its low elevation. Fly fishermen do well here on a windy day with a winged ant pattern.

Johnson Creek

A drive up road 21 easterly from Highway 12, provides anglers access to Johnson Creek and a number of lakes. The creek enters the Cowlitz River not far from Packwood. It can be fished upstream and downstream from the Highway 12 bridge, where it has a few brown trout. The first approximately 5 miles of the creek upstream is deep in a canyon, accessible only by major bushwhacking. Anglers should be aware that the canyon is deep enough in some spots that it is not possible to wade either upstream or downstream. Upstream from the canyon, it is much more accessible from the road.

A sizeable clear-flowing stream, except during heavy runoff, Johnson Creek is high-gradient in places and has limited holding water. A close examination of a contour map and bushwhacking to reach a flatter spot provides a very enjoyable day's fishing for rainbow and cutthroat, 6-10 inches. A spur road to the right just past Glacier Creek crosses Johnson Creek and allows access here. It is heavily fished at this point and upstream or downstream bushwhacking a half mile or so can provide much better fishing. Selective fishery regulations apply to Johnson Creek.

Glacier Lake (3019)

Deep 20 acre Glacier Lake was formed by a landslide, is very steep-sided and is not really fishable from shore early in the summer, except in a couple of small spots. The number of downed trees in the lake, all of which have seemingly floated to the shallow end, make access to any open water nearly impossible early in the season and it is not recommended that anglers attempt to walk out on the floating logs. When the lake drops substantially, the logs become high and dry and it is much more fishable. It produces abundant brook trout in the 7-10 inch range. It is reached by hiking 2 moderately strenuous miles on the Glacier Lake Trail, in the Goat Rocks Wilderness. Drive south approximately 5 miles up Rd. 21 off Highway 12 to Rd. 2110 then to the trailhead.

Wright Lake.

Wright Lake (3100)

Wright lake is a lovely 3.5 acre lily pad pond. Though easily reached from Rd. 21, it is capable of producing large fish, probably due to the difficulty of fishing the lake because of shoreline cover. It is stocked with cutthroat which average a fat 8-10 inches. Once the lily pads grow in earnest, a float tube or raft is a necessity.

Hugo Lakes

Lower Hugo (4000) and Upper Hugo (4100) are very small ponds, barely more than an acre each. The upper lake feeds the lower lake and neither is more than 5 feet deep. Both have produced trout historically but have fragile populations of cutthroat, which should be released. Eastern brook have also been reported. No hike is required to fish them as they are next to Rd. 21 just before it forks toward Chambers Lake and Walupt Lake. On a clear day there is an inspiring view of Mt. Rainier looking from Upper Hugo down the valley toward Lower Hugo.

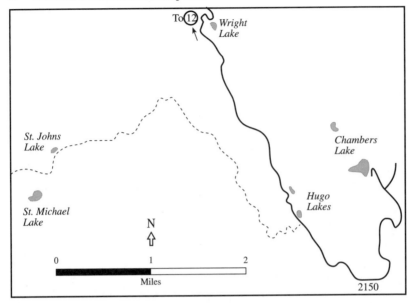

Chambers Lake (4400)

A 14 acre, 40 foot deep lake, Chambers contains 7-9 inch brook trout. It is heavily fished but a good lake to keep trout for dinner and breakfast, as the population cannot be fished out and pressure can result in larger fish. There are sometimes a few lunker brown trout, which are stocked occasionally to crop the brookies. Continue past Hugo Lake on Rd. 21 then left on 2150, following it all the way to the lake.

Walupt Lake (3927)

A very large 384 acre and 200 foot deep lake, motors allowed, 10 mph speed limit. Selective fishing only with special regulations, it is a long drive on Rd. 21 then 2160 to the lake. The lake is not stocked and cutthroat and rainbow reproduce successfully in the inlets, which are closed to fishing.

Snyder Lake (2038)

This small 3 acre lake is ice-free by the beginning of fishing season and affords anglers the opportunity to fish for brook trout, average size 8 inches. It is heavily fished despite difficult casting conditions. A Forest Service employee reports observing a very large brookie or possibly brown trout, probably 4 pounds, while paddling a canoe on the lake. He was looking for lures on the bottom when he saw a length of fishing line, which began to move. At the other end of it was a lure in the mouth of an enormous trout, cruising the lake. The lake is accessible by Rd. 1260 from the ranger station at Packwood. Stop at milepost 3 and walk over a small rise to the lake.

Art Lake (3760)

A 14 foot deep 1.5 acre lake, Art drains to Lake Creek and then the Cowlitz River. Rd. 4830 passes the lake on its north shore. This road is reached by traveling from the Packwood Ranger Station on Rd. 1260 past Snyder Lake then right on Rd. 4830 to Art Lake. It is hard to find. This somewhat boggy lake is productive and provides a good fishery for cutthroat. Anglers will continue to have good fishing here if they limit their catch and keep one fish at most. There is another small 1 acre lake a few hundred feet to the south, connected by a stream and draining to Art Lake. Art is regularly planted with cutthroat.

Packwood Lake.

Packwood Lake (2857)

Packwood Lake, more than 400 acres and 110 feet deep, has been carefully studied by fisheries biologists. It is believed that its rainbow are a unique strain. No fish have been stocked since 1965, and the tributaries are closed to fishing. Despite considerable pressure to stock the lake, the State has wisely decided to simply protect this unique population and allow it to reproduce. Concern has been

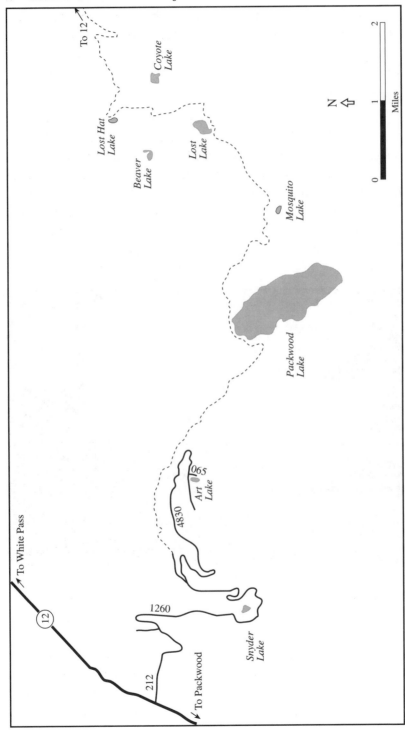

expressed about the capacity of the natural reproduction to keep up with the number of fish taken from this lake every year. Consequently, selective fishery regulations apply and no bait is allowed. The average rainbow here is approximately 9-11 inches and larger ones are plentiful, providing excellent fishing at times. Packwood Lake Trail No. 78 begins at the end of Rd. 1260 and reaches the lake in 4.6 miles. There are two unnamed lakes south of the trail to Packwood lake. There is no information regarding trout populations in either of them.

Lost Lake (5100)

No longer "lost" because it is accessible by trail from several directions, including, most commonly by passing Packwood Lake on Tr. 78, a total of 9.5 miles from the trailhead; the Bluff Lake Trail, Tr. 65, a total of 7.6 miles from the trailhead off Rd. 4612, or yet another direction, from Rd. 46 on the Clear Fork Trail, Tr. 76, past Lost Hat Lake, to Tr. 78, over 8 miles. All the hikes are very scenic. The lake produces cutthroat from 8-14 inches.

Lost Hat Lake (5520)

A small, less than 3 acre, 15 foot deep lake, it drains to Lava Creek and the Clear Fork. From Lost Lake, Tr. 78 continues two very difficult miles to Lost Hat. It is more easily accessible by hiking in from Bluff Lake, or from the Clear Fork Trail, Tr. 76. Sometimes not free of ice until August, this lake produces cutthroat to 12 inches.

Willame Lake (3650)

Fishermen reach this 7 acre, 18 foot deep lake by driving Rd. 52 from Packwood to Rd. 47, then Rd. 4730, sometimes impassable, to Rd. 042, to the gate, where it has been wisely decided that visitors must walk approximately a mile to the lake. In 1986 a 15 inch minimum size limit along with a bait ban was established in the hopes that this popular lake would produce quality fishing for anglers. Initially, there was resistance to these rules but increasing acceptance has made for excellent fishing at times.

Long Lake (3920)

A series of logging roads lead to Long Lake, which is 7 acres and 14 feet deep. The lake drains to Willame Creek. Any trout popu-

lation in the lake is dependent upon stocking. Drive Rd. 52 from
Packwood to Rd. 47 past the turnoff to Rd. 4730, then left on Rd.
4740 and drive to the north side of this narrow lake.

Skate Creek

From Packwood, paved Rd. 52 reaches Skate Creek in a few
miles, then parallels the creek upstream, coming out eventually next
to the Nisqually River, not far from Longmire. The State annually
stocks Skate Creek with catchable size trout as part of a mitigation
program with Tacoma City Light. Fish the slow-moving waters, as
the hatchery fish are used to this kind of flow. It is clear-flowing, one
of the creeks which can be fished early. It is worth taking your kids,
that is if you can find where the hatchery fish were planted. Otherwise, this is a rather difficult creek to fish, with lots of large boulders
and rough going.

For a considerable distance above its junction with the Cowlitz,
the lower reach of Skate Creek flows a distance from the road in a
valley and access is difficult. This area may be worthy of the effort to
fish it. Above its junction with Johnson Creek, its flow is reduced by
nearly half and there are many miles of fishable water above this
point. Bushwhacking will yield small trout, primarily cutthroat in
this stretch. Stopping along the road where everyone else does, puts
you in water that is too heavily fished.

Skate Creek Cuttrhoat.

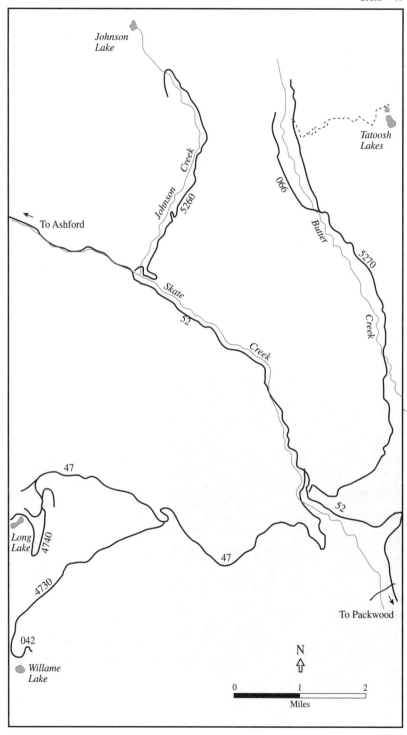

Johnson
Lake

Tatoosh
Lakes

Johnson Creek

5260

066

Butter

5270

Creek

To Ashford

Skate

52

Creek

47

Long
Lake

4740

47

52

4730

042

To Packwood

Willame
Lake

N

0   1   2
Miles

Butter Creek

Rd. 52 from Packwood, the Skate Creek Road takes anglers to a right turn onto Rd. 5270 and Butter Creek. Drive just over three miles to a bridge crossing the creek and fish upstream from here. Drive farther up the road and work your way down through the woods to the creek and you will have a pleasant day fishing for 6 to 10 inch trout. At some points the road is simply too far away from the creek to make a trip through the woods really worth it, but there are plenty of spots to provide any angler reasonable access to a fairly sizable creek with nice mountain trout. After a few miles, the road comes back to the creek, considerably smaller but still fishable. It holds rainbow and cutthroat. Selective fishery rules apply.

Johnson Lake (4500)

Accessible by traveling up the Skate Creek Road, Rd. 52, then Rd. 5260 to Rd. 5262 to its end, then by an extremely steep bushwhack, this shallow 8 acre lake is infrequently visited. It is located within the Tatoosh Wilderness Area. Its cutthroat, which run 8-10 inches and larger, are evidently able to reproduce with some success. As with many mountain lakes, it is best to carefully examine a contour map,

and if possible, bushwhack along the outlet stream. Map and compass required. Northwest of Johnson Lake are two small ponds, and upper Johnson Lake lies approximately a mile cross country to the north. There is no information available about any of them. Extreme caution should be exercised if attempting to reach these lakes.

Upper and Lower Tatoosh Lakes (5000)

Upper Tatoosh Lake, 10 acres and 38 feet deep, feeds Lower Tatoosh, 2.5

Un-named lake north of Tatoosh Lake.

acres and 23 feet deep, by a short channel. Drive Rd. 52 to Rd. 5270 then to the trail, Tr. 160. This is a difficult trail to follow, with an elevation gain of 2,400 feet. The hiking distance to these very scenic lakes is approximately 5.5 miles. The lakes have limited numbers of naturally reproducing cutthroat.

Cliffhanger Lake (4400)

This unnamed 2 acre lake, dubbed Cliffhanger by fisheries biologists due to its location, provides cutthroat. Within the Tatoosh Wilderness, it lies approximately 0.5 miles north of the smaller of the two Tatoosh lakes. Access is extremely difficult and it is not recommended that anglers attempt to find this lake unless using extreme caution and with the best equipment, maps, and compass. There is also an unnamed lake approximately 1 mile to the southeast of the Tatoosh lakes, but no fishing information is available.

Clear Fork Cowlitz River

The lower part of the beautiful Clear Fork is most easily fished by starting in the La Wis Wis campground and fishing upstream, under the Highway 12 bridge on up until it becomes too difficult to continue. It then enters a steep walled canyon. The upper stretch of the Clear Fork winds temptingly below for several miles as Highway 12 heads east from its junction with the Cayuse Pass Highway. The first formal access is off Highway 12 from the trailhead of Tr. 76, found 17 miles east of Packwood. The trail heads very steeply down to the river. Fish up or down from this point, but to reach more remote and less fished water, ford the river and continue up the trail, then turn left on Tr. 61 and hike about as far as you like once the trail comes back to the river.

Alternatively, hike from the end of Rd. 46 to Lily Lake continuing approximately another half mile or more beyond Lily Lake. There one reaches the free, but not worth it, Skeeter Shelter, where an evening's stay is the equivalent of voluntarily providing an all-night meal to the little zingers. The only alternative is complete, full-body spray with Off about every 20 minutes throughout the night. From this junction, the Clear Lost trial leads to the left and in approximately 1 mile to the Clear Fork of the Cowlitz. The river at this point is about all one could ask of a trout stream. It has beautiful pools, numerous riffles and pocket water is clear and is easily wadeable. Some report catching trout to 16 inches, others being skunked.

It is possible that the trout move up and down this river as they do in certain other streams and a good deal of hunting for them is necessary. It is seldom fished in these upper areas, because access is available only by trail.

Bluff Lake (3900)

Bluff Lake.

Within the Goat Rocks Wilderness, 8 acres and 33 feet deep, Bluff Lake is accessible from Rd. 46 off Highway 12 south of La Wis Wis campground, then on Rd. 4610 to the trailhead. A pleasant 2 mile trail, elevation gain 900 feet, leads to the lake. It contains both brook trout and cutthroat, with brookies averaging 8-11 inches and the cutthroat 8-12 inches. Persistent littering of the lake has caused the Forest Service to consider limiting use. There is quite a good fishery available if anglers will simply take care of the resource and leave no trace. This lake contains substantial numbers of freshwater shrimp, which, in combination with the lake's relatively low elevation, substantial littoral zone, abundant organic debris plus apparent reduced spawning success for brook trout, produces substantial numbers of good size trout.

Lily Lake (3700)

A flat, easy 1.3 mile hike leads from the end of Rd. 46 from Highway 12 to this sizable 25 acre, shallow lake. If ever a lake ex-

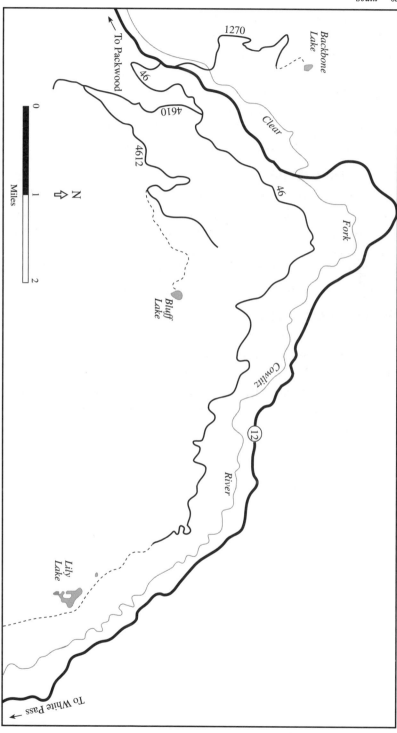

isted which could only be fished from a floating device, this is the one. The lake is eutrophying and requires a serious slog through its swampy shore to get a float tube or raft into the water, at least until the water drops and the shore dries out, if ever. The lake has been subject to winterkill but has historically provided decent trout fishing, sometimes depending upon stocking. About 0.25 miles before reaching Lily there is a small pond off to the right which can be fished more readily from shore but may not contain trout.

Coyote Lake (5100)

Four acres deep and very scenic, Coyote is the headwater of its namesake creek, which drains southeasterly to the Clear Fork. Hike past Lily Lake approximately 1 mile, turn onto Tr. 76 and travel west approximately 3 miles, then very carefully cross country from Tr. 76 to the lake. Map and compass required. The lake contains cutthroat and fishing has been reported to be quite good at times.

Backbone Lake (2050)

A small 3.5 acre lake but very deep, this is a popular hiking and fishing destination because it is an easy 0.5 mile hike, elevation gain 300 feet. Take Rd. 1270 south of La Wis Wis Campground off Highway 12 to the trailhead. Backbone is an eastern brook lake capable of producing larger than average trout, ranging from 8 to reportedly as big as 16 inches on occasion. Since the lake contains crayfish, fly anglers using a crayfish imitation might surprise themselves with a lunker brookie here. The lake is heavily used and there are only a few good places to fish from shore.

East

The western rim of the shelf dropped off 1000 feet or more in a steep incline to a tangle of wilderness. Mount Rainier rose over us. We commanded the whole scene as if we were on the roof of a cathedral. No more perfect place to camp on a clear August night could ever be found. Here we threw off our packs.

William O. Douglas

Chinook Pass

Deadwood Lakes (5300) (RNP)

Located north of Chinook Pass within the boundary of Mt. Rainier National Park, Upper Deadwood, 6 acres and Lower Deadwood, 7 acres, are connected by a stream. Hike the Pacific Crest Trail north approximately 0.5 miles looking for a way trail up to the low point in the ridge to the north and then hike cross country another 0.5 to 1 mile over the ridge to the lakes. Contour map and compass required. The lakes have historically produced cutthroat but are subject to winterkill.

Sheep Lake (5300)

Sheep is a 3 acre, 12 foot deep, eastern brook lake, with many pan-size fish. The lake is heavily used due to the short, 2.5 mile, 400 foot elevation gain hike north on the Pacific Crest Trail from the parking lot at Chinook Pass. The scenery alone makes this a great day trip.

Placer Lake (5380)

This 5 acre very shallow lake was built long ago by miners, who engineered a wood dam and a berm constructed of logs and dirt to make the lake. It can produce large trout and is regularly stocked with cutthroat. Limit the number of fish you keep and there will continue to be good size trout in the lake. To fish it, hike the Pacific Crest Trail 0.8

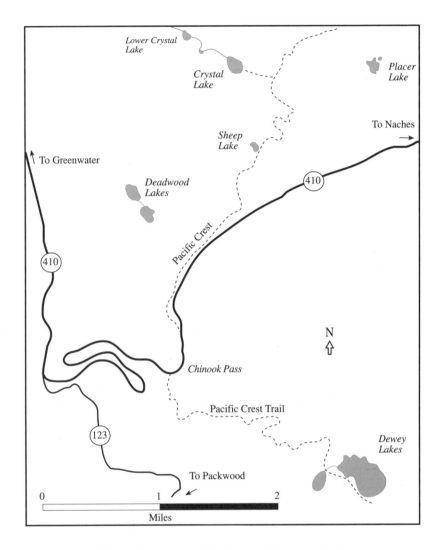

miles beyond Sheep Lake to slightly beyond Sourdough Gap, just over three very pleasant miles from the trailhead, to where Placer Lake can be seen 700 feet downhill.

Dewey Lakes (5200)

Heavily visited, 2.7 miles by trail from Tipsoo Lake or the Pacific Crest Trail, beginning at Chinook Pass, Upper Dewey, 8 acres, flows into Lower Dewey, which is 51 acres. Both lakes contain eastern brook.

American River

American River

Just over Chinook Pass from Mt. Rainier National Park, the American River flows east, until it meets the Bumping River, to form the Naches River. The American is a small river, a couple of casts across, crystal clear most of the time, but can be quite high and difficult to fish until the water level drops in July or August. It has a healthy population of cutthroat, resembling the west slope variety, rainbow and small brook trout. Whitefish are present, along with bull trout. Selective fishing regulations apply.

American River.

Heading east from Chinook Pass, the upper American River is reached by hiking on the Mesatchee Creek trail, from a marked trailhead about 6 miles east of the pass off Highway 410. A complicated trail system takes you to the river, at this point rather small, which passes through a beaver pond area containing lots of eastern brook. The river is followed farther upstream by the trail.

Approximately 8 miles east of Chinook Pass, Highway 410 reaches the river at Lodge Pole Campground. A spur road follows the river upstream a short distance. It is possible to bushwhack and wade upstream for a few miles. Downstream for several miles, the river

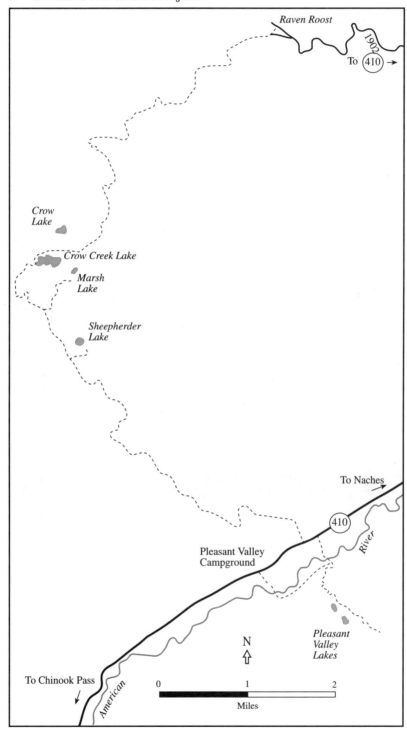

has lots of moderately fast riffle areas, with good holding water, alternating with low gradient valley stretches with long, deep holes, interspersed with shallow pea gravel and sandy runs. These low gradient areas may contain larger fish but holes are far apart in some sections and the trout are easily disturbed. Try fishing upstream from Lodge Pole Campground or fish farther downstream where you find pocket water, particularly below Pleasant Valley.

At least 12 miles of road follow the river to its junction with the Bumping River, allowing plenty of access and many good campgrounds as well. American River trout are not large—a 12 incher is a lunker—but the variety makes fishing a pleasure. Anglers have the best success a distance from the campgrounds along the river.

Pleasant Valley Lake.

Pleasant Valley Lakes

Anglers can day hike from Pleasant Valley Campground to two very small, 1 acre lakes. North Pleasant Valley Lake (3940) is 2.5 miles by trail from Pleasant Valley Campground. This lake, though regularly planted with cutthroat, appears to have some natural reproduction. The inlet on the southwest side and the outlet possibly provide spawning habitat. Stay out of these areas and let these fish reproduce if they can. South Pleasant Valley Lake (4185), more a shallow pond than a lake, requires a bushwhack and map and compass. A restricted limit would be helpful as it can only handle limited fishing pressure. With care from anglers, it can produce good-sized trout, both rainbow and cutthroat.

Little Naches River

The Little Naches River Road, Rd. 19, follows the river, leading to Rd. 1902 which travels past Huckleberry Campground to Raven Roost the trailhead to several lakes, some of which are not named on any map and require map, compass, and cross country hiking with good navigation skills.

Little Naches River.

Little Naches River

This picturesque small river is literally pounded by fishermen because there are so many campgrounds and a well-maintained road along its length. The area is heavily used by ORVs and the impact upon the river is obvious. There is an ongoing attempt to assist returning anadromous fish, including the installation of a fish ladder approximately 4 miles up the road. A section of the river benefits from selective fishing regulations, but catch and release might be a better option, at least until the resident trout population restores itself. Presently, aside from a few sections which flow through boulder and plunge pool habitat, anglers must get as far away from the road, campgrounds and ORV trails to find fair fishing for small cutthroat, rainbow and cuttbows.

Crow Lake (4800)

By hiking 3.5 miles by trail from the trailhead off Rd. 1902 near Raven Roost then 0.75 miles cross country with the assistance of a map and compass, anglers reach Crow Lake, also known as Anna Lake. It is 1900 feet north of Crow Creek Lake. Shallow and therefore subject to winterkill, it is otherwise a quite productive 3 acre lake. Crow Lake trout have historically grown to good size.

Crow Creek Lake (4540)

Pretty much a 13 acre wide spot on Crow Creek, gradually filling in, this is a productive lake, containing cutthroat and rainbow, with the cutthroat naturally reproducing. The spawning areas, at the outlet and inlet, deserve special care by all. The trout are not large, with few more than 12 inches, but there are many from 8-11 inches.

Crow Creek Lake.

Fenner Lake (5460)

Not named on maps, this lake is sometimes barren of fish due to winterkill but it is periodically planted with cutthroat. It is 3 acres, about 1.5 miles northwest of Crow Lake and fed by small pond 1100 feet west. Approximately 4 miles from the trailhead at Raven's Roost, Fenner requires map, compass and cross country hiking to find.

Janet Lake (5032)

This 4 acre crescent-shaped cutthroat trout lake, lies about 3400 feet northwest of and drains to Crow Creek Lake. It is 2.5 miles southwest of Raven's Roost Lookout, not named on any map and requires map, compass and navigation skills to find.

Rae Lake (5020)

Also known as Louise Lake, it is 20 feet deep and lies 350 feet east from the north end of Janet Lake. Along with Janet Lake, it is difficult to fish from shore. It contains cutthroat.

Marsh Lake (4670)

This 1 acre pond about 1000 feet south of Crow Creek Lake is not believed to hold trout.

Sheepherder Lake (4931)

Seven acres, 28 feet deep, Sheepherder Lake drains to Crow Creek and lies 0.75 miles south of Crow Creek Lake. It is within the boundaries of the Norse Peak Wilderness Area. Hike beyond Crow Creek Lake to the junction with trial 953 and head south to Sheepherder Lake. A steeper route exists from Highway 410 beginning on the north side of the highway east of Pleasant Valley Campground. There is adequate spawning habitat, primarily in the outlet and one should not enter the outlet stream. There are also springs in the lake of the kind that can provide, in rare situations, functional spawning for trout other than brook trout. Some cutthroat in the lake reach 12-14 inches.

Bumping River

The Bumping Lake Road, Rd. 18, begins approximately 19 miles east of Chinook Pass off Highway 410.There are 11 miles of road following the Bumping River upstream from just above its junction with the American River to Bumping Lake.

Bumping River

Below Bumping Lake the river is fast moving, has a high gradient in most places and holding water is spaced far apart. It can also be running very full into late summer, as its flow is controlled primarily for agricultural needs downstream from the Naches River. It does hold some sizable cutthroat and small rainbow.

The upper Bumping River flows into the lake at the west end and is reached by Rd. 1800. A trail follows the river upstream, passing a beautiful falls in 0.5 miles. There is no bridge across the river and from here hikers must wade across to the trail on the other side. About 0.25 miles upstream there is another scenic falls. Despite its pristine water and good flow with lots of holding water, the river seems to afford relatively poor trout fishing. Much of it flows through bedrock, seems to be regularly scoured by heavy flows and is suspiciously free of algae. Knowledgeable anglers may find a long hike up the river rewarding in its upper reaches.

Falls on the Upper Bumping River.

Bumping Lake

Bumping Lake is a very large reservoir, well known for its kokanee fishing. The kokanee are so numerous that the State has liberalized its normal lake fishing regulations to allow anglers to chum for and keep 16 Kokanee. It also has a large population of bull trout and is closed to harvest of these fish. The most popular means of fishing in this very large body of water is trolling, using pop gear and worms, flashers, and fly/maggot combinations.

Deep Creek

Deep Creek road, Rd. 1808, heads off from the Bumping Lake road, Rd. 1800, up the creek to trails to several lakes and lots of fishing opportunities. The creek itself has been closed to fishing from the mouth to the second bridge crossing Rd. 1808, 3.7 miles, to protect spawning and rearing bull trout. Above this point, it contains small brook trout.

Twin Sisters Lakes

Take the Deep Creek road, Rd. 1808 to its end at Deep Creek Campground and hike an easy 500 foot elevation gain in 1.5 miles to 31 acre Twin Sister Lake (5190). There is a trail which allows fishing access around the entire lake. It has many bays and rocky promontories, allowing for easy fishing from shore. Another 0.5 mile walk takes you to big Twin Sister (5152), a very large mountain lake at 104 acres and 55 feet maximum depth. Both lakes have nice sandy beaches and can be very crowded. There are abundant campsites and both lakes show signs of overuse. Conscientious hikers will pick up trash often left here. Eastern brook ranging 6-10 inches populate both lakes in abundance, with Little Twin Sister reported to have some larger brookies, and they are good lakes in which to keep trout, as there is no way in which even the most successful anglers could fish them out.

Round Lake (5250)

This 1 acre shallow pond is not believed to hold fish.

East Blankenship Lake (Chris Axling photo).

Blankenship Lakes

There are three Blankenship Lakes of interest to anglers, sur-

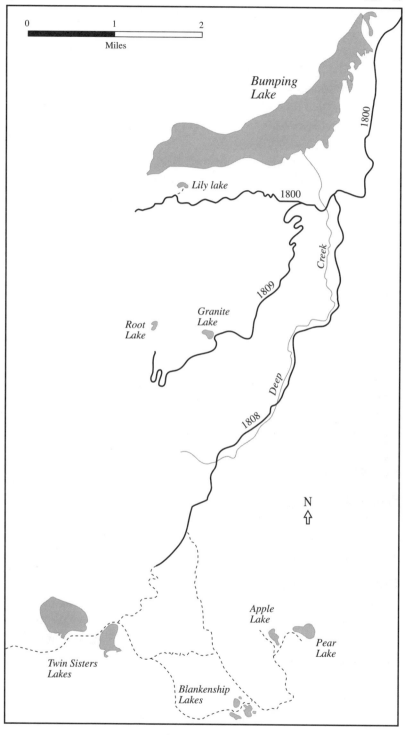

rounded by a number of small ponds. The trail "system" in this area is very confusing, with many dead-end trails. East Blankenship (5230), 10 acres and 20 feet deep, is the largest of the three, with two islands and a pretty campsite on a large rock overlooking the lake on the western shore. Although not numerous, 12-14 inch cutthroat are caught by skilled fly fishermen. It is most easily reached by a complicated route east of Little Twin Sister Lake, a total of 3.5 miles by trail from Deep Creek Campground, or from Indian Creek trail off Highway 12, but considerably further. North Blankenship (5260) 4 acres, 11 feet deep, is the smallest of the three and is a total of 3.1 miles by trail. It provides a cutthroat population similar to that of East Blankenship, but has been known to produce the largest trout of the three lakes, to 17 inches. South Blankenship (5268) 7 acres, 3.3 miles by trail, but not visible from the trail, is less frequently visited. Along with the other Blankenship Lakes, it is regularly stocked with cutthroat and has yielded large trout in the past.

Apple Lake (5060)

Seven to 8 inch brook trout are abundant in this 9 acre, very shallow lake. Accessible either by a long hike from Bumping Lake or by trail 2 miles from Blankenship Lakes, a total of 5.5 miles from Deep Creek Campground, it is essentially a wide spot in the stream, very marshy, and produces enormous quantities of mosquitoes at times. The best fishing is in the smaller part of the lake near the outlet, as the stream flowing through it creates a channel, deepest at this point.

Pear Lake (5060)

The outlet creek from Pear runs through Apple Lake, which is situated 0.25 miles west. Pear produces a population of healthy 8-9 inch eastern brook and puts out a good sized fish from time to time.

Granite Lake (5035)

At 7 acres, 13 feet deep, located next to a road, this lake provides decent fishing for brook trout, 9-12 inches. A visit to this lake though can be disheartening because of the lack of care for the surrounding environment exercised by visitors, littering the area far beyond an acceptable degree. If your vehicle is up to it, take Rd. 1809 south from the Bumping Lake road, Rd. 1800, and find Granite Lake on the right side next to the road after approximately 2.5 miles.

Root Lake (5300)

Root Lake.

Root Lake is 5 acres, 20 feet deep, located by a bushwhack of 0.75 miles, just over a ridge from road access and Granite Lake. Continue on Rd. 1809 past Granite Lake to the road end. Walk a steep 400 feet up and 300 feet down to the lake in a total of 0.6 miles. Map and compass required. It is a steep downhill slog to the lake, and this deters most fishermen. It does, however, provide good fishing for stocked rainbow in an inspiring location.

Lily lake (3860)

Lily is a 5 acre moderately deep lake which features a nice island with a campsite. It has historically been stocked with brook trout, which for some reason have had difficulty reproducing and it is periodically stocked with cutthroat. Lily has produced lunker brookies on occasion, but generally the fish are 8-9 inches. Take Rd. 1800 on the south side of Bumping Lake to within nearly 1 mile of its end and locate off to the right, short Tr. 988, 0.3 to Lily Lake. This is an easy walk with a float tube.

Cedar Lake (5260) & Little Cedar Lake (4750)

These two lakes are not particularly close to eachother and map and compass are required to find them. One route is about 2 miles cross country up the north side of Cedar creek from Tr. 971 at the end of Bumping Lake, to Little Cedar, a 3 acre lake. The long route, but trail nearly all the way, takes the hiker to Cedar, by hiking past Swamp Lake 4.6 mile from the trailhead at the end of Rd. 1800, then north on Tr. 958 for nearly 2 miles and steeply, carefully downhill to 8 acre Cedar Lake. Located in a steep walled pocket, Cedar is deep and feeds the lower lake. Both lakes hold cutthroat.

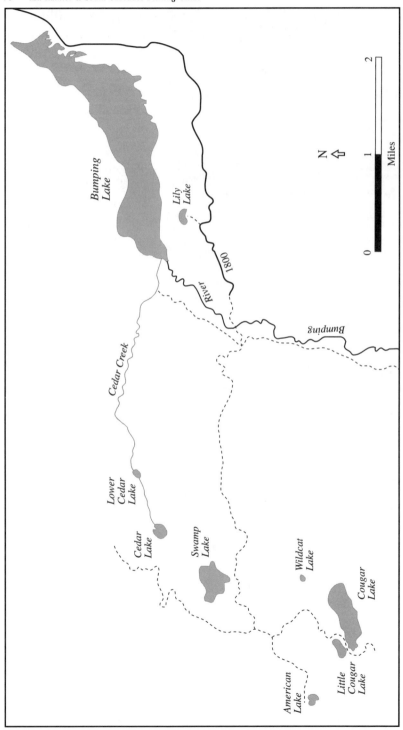

Swamp Lake (4797)

This large 51 acre lake features eastern brook along with some rainbow and is found at the end of an enjoyable 4.0 mile hike, elevation gain 1200 feet. The trail begins at the Swamp Lake trailhead, Tr. 970, at the end of Rd. 1800. Fishing is challenging from shore.

Cougar Lakes.

Cougar Lakes (5020)

Big Cougar Lake, 82 acres, 109 feet deep, the largest lake in the William O. Douglas Wilderness Area, is 2 miles by trail past Swamp Lake, a total of 6.3 miles from the trailhead at the end of Bumping Lake. It contains a naturally reproducing brook trout population and a few rainbow, but produces little food for trout and consequently its trout tend to be stunted. Little Cougar Lake, 13 acres, 26 feet deep, connected by a small neck of land, also has a large population of small brook trout from 2-8 inches. There is an unnamed lake to the east of Cougar Lakes that may be worth investigating.

Wildcat Lake (5200)

Situated on a bench about 0.5 miles north, cross country and uphill from the Big Cougar Lake outlet, this 1.5 acre lake holds stocked rainbow. Map and compass required, although there is somewhat of a trail.

American Lake.

American Lake (5260)

Accessible from the trailhead at the end of Bumping Lake or by hiking 3.5 miles from the Dewey Lakes, this 3.5 acre lake is 14 feet deep. It is easily fished, and contains small to medium length cutthroat.

Naches River

The Naches is a large, beautiful river, very appealing to anglers, with excellent riffles, holding water, pools, runs, all a fly fisherman could ask. It looks great, but how good is trout fishing? Locals will tell you, not very good. It holds good numbers of small fish, lots of minnows, and a few large fish. If this river held trout in even half the number and size of the Yakima River, it would be a very fine fishing destination. Just the look of it makes you want to fish it.

Anglers willing to put in the time have found cutthroat to 18-19 inches in the deep parts of the upper river and some sizable rainbow here and there, particularly below the river's junction with the Tieton. Weighted nymphs and streamers are much more productive for these big trout than dry flies. It is possible that through new regulations, trout in this river may return to the size old-timers fondly recall.

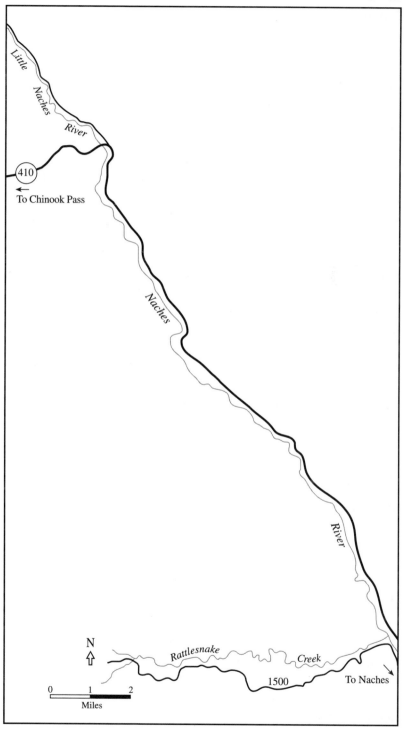

Little Naches River

410

← To Chinook Pass

Naches

River

N
↑

0   1   2
Miles

Rattlesnake   Creek

1500

To Naches

Rattlesnake Creek

Take Nile Road from Highway 410, crossing a beautiful stretch of the Naches River, turn onto Rd. 1500, which initially parallels the creek at its level, and then travels high above it, providing access to miles of the creek. The road wanders far away from the creek in many places, but there are a few rough access roads along the way. At approximately 9 miles the road dips down toward the creek and crosses it shortly. Just before this crossing there is a rough road 0.5 miles to Rattlesnake Springs, which also provides access. This area is more heavily fished than the rest of the creek, but there is fair to good fishing in any given hole for fish 6 to an occasional 16 inches. There is a good distance between holes though, and walking is necessary, but you will not mind it through this beautiful country. Provided you do not risk your life, working your way down to any of the deeper parts of the creek can allow for good fishing.

Rattlesnake Creek is an example of what kind of fishery may result from designation as catch and release only. This is not to say that all stream fishing should be catch and release, but anglers who want quality stream fishing for trout should refer to Rattlesnake Creek, the Yakima River, and other catch and release streams as very strong support for this kind of regulation in the right type of stream. Other states have increasingly gone to catch and release and slot limits, and Washington State is beginning to see the wisdom in these policies.

Mt. Rainier National Park
East: Cayuse Pass

State Route 123, the Cayuse Pass highway, provides access to the eastern edge of Mt. Rainier National Park, and a number of streams and several lakes which border the park.

Chinook Creek (RNP)

As lovely a stream as one can find anywhere, Chinook Creek is a clear flowing creek about a long cast across in most places. It is formed by the junction of Kotsuck, Dewey and Deer Creeks. All three hold trout but they are much more abundant in Kotsuck. A short downhill trail off SR 123 originates just south of the point where the highway crosses Deer Creek and leads to the junction. Here the

Eastside Trail follows Chinook Creek, crossing it at a waterfall, then downstream to its mouth on the Ohanepacosh River, ending at the Ohanepacosh Campground. The creek is home to at least two strains of cutthroat, one resembling the coastal variety, the other a west slope cutthroat similar to those in Idaho and Montana. There are also cuttbows and rainbow, with the largest trout about 12-14 inches. There are few large trout in this stream but you can have a very pleasant day fishing it. Along with Kotsuck, Dewey and Deer creeks, it is restricted to fly fishing only.

Ohanepacosh River.

Ohanepacosh River (RNP)

There are few rivers in this world more stunningly beautiful than the Ohanepacosh River. It is crystal clear, with ice blue pools, every rock, stick and leaf visible on the bottom—it holds no secrets below its surface, except one. Why doesn't it have more trout? It may be that it is relatively sterile, like ice, and does not support enough food to adequately nourish very many trout. The river is very cold, so growth rates are slow.

Few anglers report great success in the river but some claim that there are reasonable numbers of small rainbow in the lower reaches and cutthroat and brook trout higher up. Some dry fly anglers tell of good dry fly fishing with attractors such as Wulf patterns beginning in mid-August through early October. If for no other reason than to see it close up, it may be worth exploring by anglers with the inclination to do some investigating. It has long been a fly fishing only stream.

Laughingwater Creek (RNP)

Anglers can reach good lake fishing from the Laughingwater Creek trailhead on Cayuse Pass Highway, route 123, making a return trip to the trailhead or continuing on and out at Chinook Pass, Bumping Lake or several other locations.

Three Lakes (4850) (RNP)

Just within the eastern boundary of Mt. Rainer National Park, lie two rather deep 4 acre lakes and one shallow 2 acre lake. They are 5.5 miles from the trailhead, nearly 3000 feet in elevation gain. There are no fish reported in the lakes.

One Lake (5050)

Very small 2 acres, 9 feet deep, One Lake's outlet flows into Red Rock Creek. It is regularly stocked with cutthroat trout. Continue 1 mile beyond Three Lakes, turn north on the Pacific Crest Trail for approximately 0.5 miles, about 7 miles from the Laughingwater Creek trailhead on Highway 123, then cross country east, as there is no very well established trail. Map and compass required.

Two Lake (5390)

Also known as Red Rock Lake, as it is the headwater of Red Rock Creek, 3 acre Two Lake offers good cutthroat fishing at times. It is named Two Lake because of the small pond to the south. It lies next to the Pacific Crest Trail approximately 1 mile north of the Laughingwater Creek trail junction with the Crest trail, slightly over 7 miles from the trailhead.

Carlton Creek

The Carlton Creek Road, Rd. 44, takes off SR 123 approximately 2 miles north of the junction of SR123 and Highway 12. The creek holds small rainbow, cutthroat and whitefish. At the end of the road, there are trails to several lakes offering good fishing.

Fish Lake (4200)

Within the William O. Douglas Wilderness, this lake has a pre-

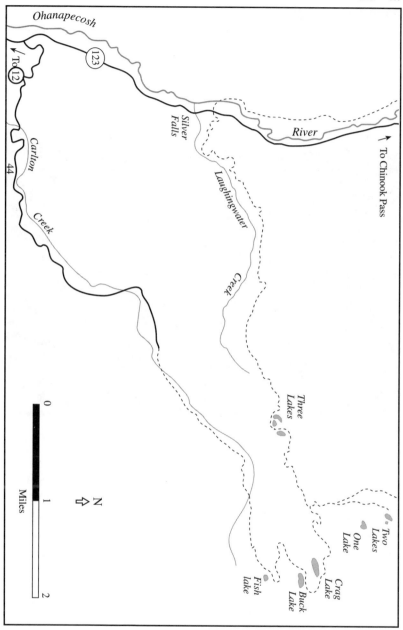

dominately brook trout population of pan-sized fish but also produces cutthroat trout. Hike 3.7 miles on Tr. 22 from the Carlton Creek road end, elevation gain 1000 feet to this 10 acre, swampy, shallow lake.

Buck Lake (4660)

Twenty-three acre Buck Lake is reached by hiking to Fish Lake, then turning north and continuing on the Pacific Crest Trail for another mile, and finally by a 0.25 mile bushwhack. Map and compass are necessary to find the lake, which occasionally yields cutthroat to 14 inches.

Buck Lake.

Crag Lake (5020)

North of Buck Lake 0.5 miles on the Pacific Crest Trail, a total of 6 miles by trail from the trailhead at the end of the Carlton Creek road, Crag Lake is 5 acres, 21 feet deep. Along with Buck Lake, it is also accessible from the Laughingwater Creek trail beginning in Mt. Rainier National Park. Crag produces Cutthroat to 10-12 inches with a few larger. There is an unnamed lake southwest 0.5 miles from Crag.

Soda Springs

East 1.3 miles on Highway 12 beyond its junction with Highway 123, Rd. 45 takes off to the north. Follow it to a left on Rd. 4510 and drive the road approximately 5 miles to Soda Springs Campground, the trailhead for numerous lakes.

Summit Creek

At Summit Creek Campground, 2 miles in on Rd. 4510, the road crosses the creek, which flows below in a small canyon, and has good holding water. The road continues another 3 miles to Soda Springs Campground, high above the creek, meeting it just before reaching the campground. One can fish upstream or downstream in pleasant surroundings here, but it is very heavily fished near the campground, and only the most heroic trout could possibly survive in the immediate area. Bushwhacking will get you to boulder and pool areas which hold small rainbow and cutthroat.

Jug Lake (4550)

An eastern brook lake, 28 acres, 30 feet deep with a brushy shore, it is a fairly strenuous 3.2 miles by trail from Soda Springs Campground.

Chain Lakes (5000)

The Chain Lakes consist of four lakes, the largest 4 acres and the smallest 0.5 acre. All but the largest are very shallow. The largest has historically held fish, brookie and brown trout have in the past been available to anglers, but all may be barren now. They are found at the end of a short trail west of Jug Lake.

Little Snow Lake (4800)

A small, narrow 2 acre, 10 foot deep eastern brook lake, it is located about 500 feet west from Frying Pan Lake, adjacent to Tr. 43. Look for elk on this lake's southern shore.

Frying Pan Lake (4850)

Popular and fished heavily, 23 acre Frying Pan Lake is rather deep, lies in a large meadow of grass, frequented by elk herds. Somewhat marshy, the lake is surrounded by reeds with small boulders scattered along the shoreline. It is stocked with cutthroat and some very large cutthroat have been caught here. Hike beyond Jug Lake on Tr. 43, past the junction with Tr. 41, ahead on Tr. 43 for 1.4 miles to Frying Pan, passing Little Snow Lake along the way.

Jess Lake (5200)

Oblong, fairly steep sided, 0.3 miles beyond Pipe Lake, 4 acre Jess Lake is regularly planted with trout, either cutthroat or rainbow depending upon stocking policy, and may yield both from time to

Jess Lake.

time. It is capable of producing good numbers of 14-16 inch trout. Accessible from a number of trailheads, including Soda Springs, Leech Lake and Dog Lake, the shortest route is on Tr. 44, continuing east beyond Penoyer Lake for approximately 1 mile, then south on the Pacific Crest Trail about 0.2 miles, a total of roughly 6 miles from Soda Springs. The lake is visible from the trail. There are many ponds in the area as well.

Pipe Lake (5175)

About 0.5 miles south of Jess Lake, this 9 acre deep blue-green lake holds eastern brook and planted cutthroat and rainbow, depending upon the current stocking program. It is also 1 mile beyond Buesch and several unnamed lakes, all of which are reached from Leech Lake and Dog Lake.

Snow Lake (4975)

8 acres and 30 feet deep, Snow Lake lies approximately 1.5 mile east from Jug Lake and drains to Summit Creek. By trail from Soda Springs, it is a total of 5 miles, if the shortcut to the Pacific Crest Trail is utilized off Tr. 45, which takes off north from Tr. 44, 3.7 miles from Soda Springs, at the junction of Tr. 44, Tr. 41 and Tr. 45. It is regularly stocked with cutthroat. A map is useful in finding the shortest route to the lake.

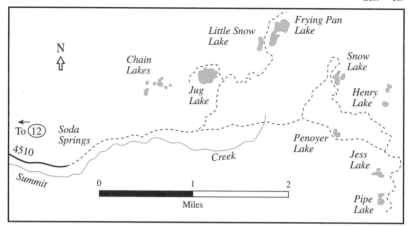

Bill Lake (5000)

Cross country east-southeast of Snow Lake there are many lakes, most of which are unnamed. Bill, at 4 acres, 30 feet deep, is a good cutthroat producer. Henry Lake (5150) a small 1.5 acre lake, is not known to hold trout. This is a great area to explore, if an ample supply of mosquito repellent is at hand.

White Pass

The White Pass area provides a great variety of high mountain lakes accessible by trail as well as some which are next to roads. While there are a few lakes to the south of the Pass, the area north of White Pass has far too many lakes and ponds to completely describe in this guidebook. The north area is reached not only from trails off Highway 12, but also from trails originating at the Deep Creek road above Bumping Lake and from Soda Springs. It is an enticing area for anglers because it has so many lakes with good fishing and many unnamed ponds and lakes containing fish, which make exploring an exciting enterprise. The area also, unfortunately, has more than an abundant number of mosquitoes during most of the summer and can cause even the most dedicated angler to itch and scratch for a week after a few days fishing the area. The following lakes are those known to hold trout and directions are intended to denote the shortest route to them.

Knuppenberg Lake (4106)

Knuppenberg Lake is fishable practically from the highway. Brown trout were planted in the late 1980's to reduce the brookie

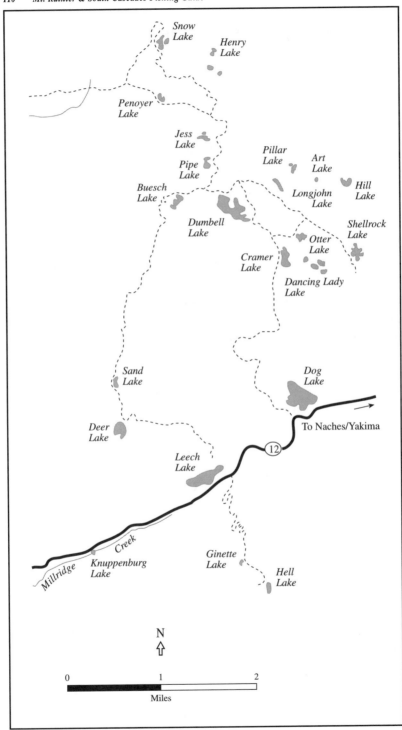

Snow Lake

Henry Lake

Penoyer Lake

Jess Lake

Pipe Lake

Buesch Lake

Pillar Lake

Art Lake

Longjohn Lake

Hill Lake

Dumbell Lake

Shellrock Lake

Cramer Lake

Otter Lake

Dancing Lady Lake

Sand Lake

Dog Lake

Deer Lake

To Naches/Yakima

Leech Lake

12

Millridge Creek

Knuppenburg Lake

Ginette Lake

Hell Lake

N

0   1   2

Miles

population. The plan has apparently succeeded as the lake has historically produced a few lunker trout, but is very heavily fished due to its location. Highway noise detracts from the fishing experience here but the brown trout are an attraction.

Brown Trout from White Pass area lake.

Leech Lake (4412)

Well known to fly fishermen, 40 acre Leech Lake has long been a fly-only lake. It is located at White Pass at the Cascade Crest. It is relatively shallow and features eastern brook, some of which can reach 16 inches. Most fish are somewhat disappointingly small. Fly anglers would do well to keep what is allowed by regulations here, as trout size will increase if the small brookies are harvested. While catch and release is certainly the best policy overall, there are a few exceptions and overpopulated brookie lakes are the leading one. Brookies are great eating as well.

Trails from Leech Lake

Most trails in this area lead to lakes to the north, but a few, along with the White Pass Ski Lift, lead to lakes south of White Pass.

Ginnette Lake (5410)

The Pacific Crest trail, Tr. 2000, runs next to Leech Lake, approximately 0.7 miles east of White Pass, near the White Pass Campground. The trail heads south to Ginnette Lake, climbing 1000 feet in 2.5 miles. It is a cutthroat trout producer but may experience winterkill.

Hell Lake.

Hell Lake (5414)

A small 3 acre, 11 foot deep lake, it is another 0.5 miles past Ginette Lake on the Pacific Crest Trail, then a bushwhack of 0.5 miles. The bushwhack may have been the origin of the name for the lake. Map and compass required. The lake supports a cutthroat trout population and can produce an occasional lunker.

Both Ginette and Hell lakes can also be reached by taking the White Pass chairlift to the top or climbing up the hill on which it is located. From there, hike east and downhill to Ginette and Hell Lakes.

Deer Lake (5206)

From the trailhead next to Leech Lake just beyond White Pass Campground, Deer Lake is a pleasant 2.7 mile walk and an 800 foot elevation gain north on the Pacific Crest trail. It is stocked with cutthroat and also contains brook trout.

Sand Lake (5295)

A short walk of 0.5 miles beyond Deer Lake, Sand Lake does not have any fish.

Buesch Lake (5081)

Slightly more than 6 miles from the trailhead at Leech Lake, or 7 miles from Dog Lake Campground, there are numerous small lakes and ponds near Buesch Lake. It is a good location from which to explore trout fishing in the area. This shallow, marshy lake contains lots of small brook trout and gazillions of mosquitoes.

Trails from Dog Lake

Dog Lake.

Dog Lake (4207)

A large, very deep 60 acre lake, Dog Lake is next to Highway 12 and is very heavily fished. However, it is planted much more frequently than other lakes in the area, including plants of 8-12 inch trout and often provides good fishing in the early mornings and evenings. It produces both rainbow and eastern brook, with some holdovers to 14 inches and larger. It is a good bet for float tube fishing and a good place to bring novice anglers.

Cramer Lake (5025)

Cramer is 19 acres, 34 feet deep. An easy 4.5 miles by trail, 800 foot elevation gain, it is the closest lake to the Dog Lake trailhead, very regularly visited and fished. Nevertheless, the lake has an abundant food supply, plentiful fresh water shrimp and can produce good-sized rainbow trout. The lake would benefit from a reduced catch limit, possibly going to a no bait fishery. The Forest Service reportedly may have to restrict access if hikers, campers, and fishermen do not take better care of the lake.

Otter Lake (5030)

Approximately 0.5 miles beyond Cramer Lake, 7 acre Otter Lake cannot be seen from the trail and requires a bushwhack of 0.5 miles to find. It is regularly stocked and despite its appearance, has produced good sized cutthroat.

Shellrock Lake (4926)

This 11 acre lake is located east of Otter Lake and is approximately 6.2 miles by trail from Dog Lake Campground. It has been known to provide very good fishing on occasion for rainbow trout. It is essentially two lakes joined by a narrow channel. Most anglers hike 1 mile beyond Otter on the trail to fish it, but it is also accessible from Tr. 1104 off Highway 12. This route is shorter at 4.8 miles, but considerably steeper.

Dancing Lady Lake.

Dancing Lady Lake (4980)

By bushwhacking 0.75 miles east, cross country from Cramer Lake, or west from Shellrock Lake, 7 acre Dancing Lady Lake can be found. It is regularly stocked with cutthroat trout.

Dumbbell Lake (5091)

On Tr. 56 5.2 miles from Dog Lake Campground, 0.7 miles northwest beyond Cramer Lake, and also 0.5 miles east of Buesch

Lake, this large 42 acre lake supports eastern brook and cutthroat to 12 inches and bigger. It drains to Buesch Lake and Summit Creek.

Long John Lake (5200)

Northwest beyond Otter Lake on Tr. 1142 approximately 1 flat mile, Long John produces cutthroat and is the gateway to many lakes which can be reached by way trails or cross country. Map and compass are necessary. These include:

Pillar (5273): 1000 feet northeast from Long John Lake, a 4 acre cutthroat lake.

Art (5230): A small 2 acre lake, 1400 feet west from Hill Lake and 1500 feet southeast from Pillar Lake, regularly stocked with rainbow.

Hill (5110): Known as a rainbow producer, Hill is 6 acres, 0.3 miles east of Art.

There are ponds and small lakes in this area too numerous to ever fish in a summer. Some are rumored to contain lunker trout.

Tieton River

Tieton River

The mainstem Tieton flows through some of the most scenic territory in Washington on its way to join the Naches River. Unfortunately for anglers, its flow is controlled for agricultural purposes from Rimrock Dam and the dramatic rise and fall of the river makes it difficult for a resident trout and anadromous fish to thrive. It is regularly stocked with 8-12 inch rainbow by WDFW though, and along with a few resident fish, it provides popular trout fishing during the summer.

Clear Lake (3615)

This large 256 acre very scenic lake provides good fishing for rainbow to 14 inches and larger along with a few brook trout. The west arm of the lake is a fine place to fish from a float tube or boat as it has numerous bays and shallow areas. The lake is large enough that it can support all types of trout fishing. Several roads lead off Highway 12 to Clear Lake.

Clear Creek

The stream flowing out of Dog Lake becomes Clear Creek and travels over an enormous falls well worth viewing from the parking

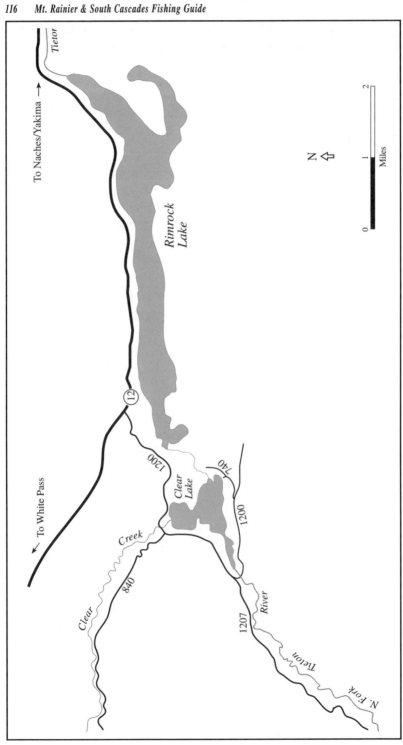

area and short trail just east of Dog Lake off Highway 410. Downstream from the falls, Clear Creek flows through a flat valley, eventually entering Clear Lake at its West end. It contains a few fish, rainbow and eastern brook, with the brookies found farther upstream toward the falls. The well-marked turnoff to Clear Lake, Rd. 1200, leaves Highway 410 and soon crosses Clear Creek. On the south side of the bridge, a road travels up the creek for a few miles until a washout makes it impassable.

North Fork Tieton River

North Fork Tieton River.

Rd. 1200 continues off Highway 410 past Clear Creek along the west arm of Clear Lake and Rd. 1207 shortly branches off, allowing access to the North Fork Tieton. From its mouth in Clear Lake, the road parallels it, too far from the river for easy access, but here and there the road comes close to the river, following it up a very scenic valley with towering mountains at the end. There are miles of river which are seldom, if ever, fished. The road is slightly over 5 miles long, and leading to the North Fork trailhead which takes you upstream to stretches that are even less often fished. The North Fork contains rainbow, cutthroat and whitefish. It has lots of log jams and snags and a low gradient but is somewhat unproductive as the numbers of trout are rather low. Insect life is limited and the trout are generally unwilling to rise to dry flies. Weighted nymphs will catch trout however and some anglers who have fished the river repeatedly report reasonably good results, especially on cutthroat. Whitefish are rather numerous and can provide enjoyable angling for those who know how to fish for them with nymphs.

Devil's Washbasin (6268)

This 2 acre cutthroat lake, is found on the northwest side of Devil's Horn Mountain, draining to the North Fork Tieton River. It is a cutthroat producer. There is no trail and finding it requires real mountaineering skills, along with map and compass.

Rimrock Lake (2918)

Rd. 12 leads south off Highway 12 to Rimrock Lake, an enormous reservoir which controls the flow of the mainstem Tieton. It produces rainbow and the naturally reproducing kokanee are abundant and provide good fishing throughout the summer months.

South Fork Tieton River

Rd. 1000 leads from the south shore of Rimrock Lake up the South Fork of the Tieton River to a number of lakes. Though a fine looking river and very tempting to anglers, the South Fork has been closed to fishing to protect bull trout.

Phantom Lake (4300)

A small 1 acre, 11 foot deep lake west of the junction of Discovery Creek and the South Fork, Phantom Lake is subject to winterkill and is dependent upon stocking for a trout population. There is an established trail 1.5 miles long from the lake to road access from a spur road off Rd. 1000.

Conrad Lakes (5293)

Anglers fish for cutthroat trout in these two 1 acre lakes, 400 feet apart. They drain to Long Creek and are at the end of Rd. 1000. Check with the Forest Service to determine road condition and access.

Surprise Lake (5300)

This 14 acre lake is located in the headwaters of the South Fork Tieton River, accessible by an approximately 4 mile hike on Tr. 1120 beginning at Conrad Meadows, far up the South Fork on Rd.1000. Surprise is a cutthroat producer.

Warm Lake (6350)

Warm Lake is a 1 acre pond lying in the headwaters of the north branch of the South Fork Tieton River. It is 1.3 miles northwest from Surprise Lake, a serious cross country trek. Map and compass required. It has been rumored to produce sizable cutthroat trout on occasion.

Cirque Lake (5650)

Seven acres, 1 mile west of Diamond Lake, at the head of Tenday Creek, Cirque Lake drains northerly to the South Fork Tieton River. It is reached by Tr. 1134 from Conrad Meadows. It is also theoretically accessible from a 4-wheel drive road ending in a trail to the lake. A map and luck are needed to find it this way. Stocked with cutthroat.

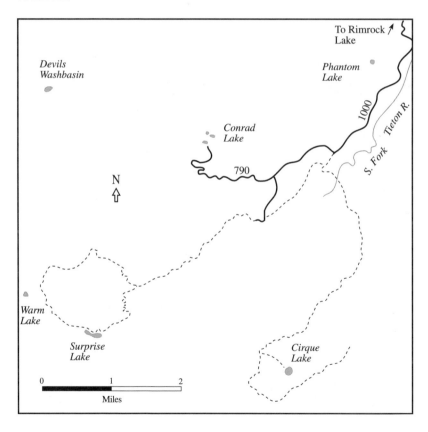

Fishing Techniques

As I walked down the grassy mountain to this lake I saw they were rising. Did you ever see a million trout rising? Well, a million trout were dimpling the surface of that lake, and I defy anyone who doubts me to go there and prove me wrong.

Ted Trueblood

Fly Fishing Mt. Rainier and South Cascade Mountain Lakes

Choosing a lake to fish is a pleasant task. Seasonal lake conditions, trout populations, casting room, difficulty in access, and availability of campsites are the primary variables to consider when planning. It is important to be mindful of the length of any hike to the lake. Anglers will want to keep weight at a minimum.

Equipment

Pack rods are highly recommended. Some four or five piece models are available at a reasonable price. Most of these fly rods can also be used as spinning rods, although with some degree of difficulty. They should be long enough to allow the shore–bound fly fisherman the necessary distance in casting to get a fly out far enough. A good alternative is to carry a 2–piece 9 foot rod in an aluminum rod case, padded on both ends to reduce shock. The rod case may be used as a staff along the trail.

The mountain lake angler will need an inexpensive small, graphite fly reel with light, 4-5 weight fly line, in interchangeable spools, both dry and sink tip.

As long and fine a leader as the angler can manage for dry fly fishing will greatly improve success. A leader of at least 12 feet is almost mandatory on most mountain lakes. The only limitation on length is whether you can effectively cast a fly with such a long leader. 6X and 7X leaders are recommended for dry fly fishing, as you will generally be using very small flies and leader visibility is always an issue. When wet fly and nymph fishing, leaders can be shortened to 8-9 feet and tippets reduced to 4x or 5x.

Years ago, anglers built rafts from materials they found at high lakes, using logs floating on the shoreline. Some even hauled in lumber, rope and nails. Paddles were crafted from small sticks or lumber. It was common to drive or hike to a high mountain lake hoping to find such a raft. They were always hard to maneuver but allowed one to get out onto the lake and cast to all parts of the lake. With the advent of spinning reels and modern fly rods and lines, mountain lakes can be fished from shore with considerable success.

If anglers are willing to carry the weight, float tubes and inflatable rafts will certainly improve their success. Lightweight float tubes,

though expensive, are available and eventually most avid alpine lake anglers will consider them part of their necessary equipment. Ultralight waders are a good choice for most long hikes, as they pack easily and allow fly fishermen to get further out into the lake, expanding the room for backcasting. Caution must be exercised entering the lake though, as you may find yourself sinking into the lake bottom and your waders filling with icy water, a truly unpleasant experience and sometimes dangerous.

Float tubing for mountain cutthroat.

Many high mountain lakes are very difficult to fish using traditional fly casting, due to precipitous shorelines, heavy vegetation, swampy edges, and shallow shelves extending well out into the lake. Because of this, it is recommended that the fly fisherman bring along an ultralight spinning reel and when necessary, fish with a couple of split shot and a wet fly or the bubble and fly technique. Most children will be unable to fish successfully from shore unless they use this technique, and even then, they need quite a lot of help. (They also like to watch a bubble float) There are exceptions where kids can readily cast flies with a fly line and fly rod, but much of the time they can't flyfish productively.

When to Fish

Obviously, one cannot fish an iced-over lake. Lower elevation mountain lakes are usually free of ice by the first week of May, but most alpine lakes are frozen in until mid-June at the earliest, the majority until July, and some are still ice-covered until August. Park Service and Forest Service rangers have the best information and an inquiry can save anglers a lot of trouble.

Most veteran high lake fishermen have favorite lakes they try to fish just at the time the ice comes off, because trout will often then go on a sustained feeding campaign. After that, fishing is generally best very early in the morning and particularly in the evening. An exception to all rules about the best time to fish is that anytime trout are actively rising, taking insects on or just below the surface, it is time to fish.

Finding the Best Fishing Locations on the Lake

Most anglers are more than ready to fish as their hike takes them within sight of a lake. If possible, before approaching the shoreline, try to determine the most likely spot to begin fishing. There are few places in the world more still than an alpine lake when the wind is not blowing. The trout in this environment are easily disturbed. If fish are rising and there is a spot nearby with good backcasting room, head for it. Otherwise, find a place where there is casting room and there is an inlet, or the lake drops off sufficiently so that you will not be casting over very shallow water.

You may decide simply to circle the lake, casting as you move around it. If so, exercise great care because mountain lake shorelines are extremely fragile and degrade easily. Generally, since trout in lakes tend to circulate, cruising the shoreline, they will come to you,

Shore fishing a South Cascade Mountain lake.

and finding a comfortable spot to cast with deep enough water will be a good choice. Rocky points jutting into the lake are good spots, as are sizable downed trees extending into the lake. Be careful, however, because trees can be slippery and will sometimes sink right under you.

Wind direction is often an important consideration in finding a good location to fish in a lake. While a steady wind will often aid in casting as long as you are casting with its direction, such a wind will sometimes blow insects toward the opposite shore, and fish will pick them off there. Strong casters often have good luck casting into the wind on the windward shore. Sometimes, though, the wind will blow insects off trees and bushes into the lake from the shoreline nearest the wind direction, and this may be productive as well. The author has experienced, for example, ant hatches where the wind blows them over the shore and into the lake, with the result that the trout feed in a frenzied, all-out manner.

How to Fish the Lake

High mountain lakes are often mirror-still, depending upon the time of day and weather. They are also nearly always perfectly clear, and anything that lands upon the surface can be readily seen by the lake's trout. Fly anglers should follow E. B. Webster's advice, applying "the art of skimming the flies out over the water so that they will settle as softly as thistle seed."

If trout are rising, an attempt should be made to "match the hatch." Failing that, Mt. Rainier and Cascade mountain lake trout respond very well to a generic small Adams, Grey or Royal Wulf, size

14-20. Avoid false casting as much as possible, and use a delicate presentation. Once the fly has landed, straighten the leader, pulling the fly line as far away from the fly as possible, and wait. As long as the fly is floating properly and fish are rising within a reasonable distance, there is no reason to lift the fly off and cast again, for every cast disturbs the fish momentarily. The best high lake dry fly anglers have a great deal of patience, particularly on calm days.

South Cascade Brook Trout.

A very effective way to catch alpine trout which are rising but will not take the offered dry fly is to use a dropper system, a series of two or three flies on the same leader, tied approximately 12 to 18 inches apart. This system allows anglers to attract trout taking emergers below the surface. Very slight movement is appropriate to represent the emerging stage of the fly. Lifting the rod occasionally will often be enough.

In the absence of fish rising, you will probably not want to fish with a dry fly. Careful examination of the shoreline may give you some idea of insect life under the surface. Attempt to imitate what you find with a nymph or wet fly. A sink tip line is often your best bet, but a dry line may be used with weighted nymphs or wet flies. The clarity of high mountain lakes allows trout to see subsurface flies from a very long distance. Thus, fishing the very bottom of the lake is not generally necessary. However, during the middle of the summer, and particularly on clear, sunny days, you will need to get down to the bottom and work the nymph slowly back to you. If nothing works just below the surface, halfway down or near the bottom, sometimes an attractor such as a Wooly Bugger or Muddler Minnow will draw a strike. These two flies are particularly effective near dark.

When traditional fly casting from the shore of a lake is simply too difficult, due to vegetation, slope, or a variety of other conditions, fly fishing can still be done effectively in such situations by using a spinning reel with a bubble and fly. Casting bubbles are generally heavy enough to allow a very long cast. Attaching a 6X or 5X leader of approximately 4 to 6 feet beyond the bubble to the fly works well. Unfortunately, the bubble often hits the water with a considerable splash. Tighten up and let it sit. It is important that there is little or no slack between the bubble and the fly. When fishing it with a nymph or wet fly, work it back very gradually.

If the bubble and fly technique does not work and you have children along, you may wish to use lures or bait, if necessary and regulations allow, to keep them interested.

Anglers using a boat or a float tube must put an extraordinary distance between themselves and their fly, as mountain lake trout are easily disturbed by the movement of water craft.

Barbless hooks should always be used. They are nearly as effective as barbed hooks and substantially reduce trout mortality.

Frying Pan Lake.

Ten Essential Flies

Anglers often carry too many flies and spend far too much time changing them. The flies listed here should allow you to catch fish in nearly all high mountain lake situations. Bringing along a few extra, of course, will probably increase your chances.

1. **Adams**—12-20.
2. **Grey or Royal Wulf** —14-20.
3. **Scud**—8-20 in a variety of colors, tan preferred.
4. **Callibaetis Nymph**—14-18.
5. **Chironomid Nymph**—10-18, in red, brown, black, tan and olive.
6. **Hare's Ear**—10-18.
7. **Midge**—16-22 in black and gray.
8. **Pheasant Tail**—14-18.
9. **Woolly Bugger**—2–6 in black, tan, olive and brown.
10. **Muddler Minnow**—6-14.

Soft hackles in a variety of colors and sizes are useful all–purpose flies and will often work with a variety of retrieves.

Fly fishing Mt. Rainier and Cascade Mountain Streams

When I reach a trout stream, a strange malady takes possession of me, and I have the delusion that the most urgent and vital thing in this world is to get into that water and start casting a fly. And that is exactly what I do. I just can't wait a minute. There is no cure for it, but there is a method that will turn the fever of enthusiasm to good use. I enter the stream below where I want to start fishing and cast to my heart's content, or until the fever subsides. In this way I get the kinks out of my system, line and leader.

Fred Everett

When to Fish

Washington State regulations control trout fishing in all Cascade and Mt. Rainier streams. Once stream fishing season begins, there is sometimes a brief period in the early part of the season when they may be fished succesfully before significant runoff. Often, however, runoff begins in earnest before the opening date, and it is seldom

Tahoma Creek is unfishable at high water.

worth fishing the streams until runoff has subsided substantially.

Inside Mt. Rainier National Park, many rivers and creeks carry large quantities of glacial flour, which cause them to be turbid much of the season. Added to this is often heavy runoff, which can make them run chocolate brown for much of at least early summer. However, there are clear-flowing streams both within and outside Mt. Rainier National Park which are fishable relatively early, provided the spring runoff has not made them rushing torrents or substantially muddied them as well. Those streams described in this guidebook which do not carry glacial flour are often fishable very early in the season. At that time, try fishing around the edges, and you will be pleasantly surprised how active the fish can be once the water temperature warms a bit.

As summer comes on, the clear-flowing streams begin to warm, reduce gradually in size, and the insects within them become quite active. Streams with glacial till generally become even more muddy as temperatures rise and are very difficult to fish. Where there are clear edges or feeder streams, there can occasionally be decent fishing, but most anglers will simply be wasting their time fishing these streams until cold nights set in again in fall. By mid-July many clear-flowing streams provide good fishing, improving into August and September, as the flows drop and fish spread throughout the streams,

Mt. Rainier Stream.

taking holding and feeding lies, familiar to all fishermen. Heavy rains during the summer can blow out a stream from time to time, but they generally subside rather quickly, and fishing becomes good as they return to normal summer condition.

In the fall, as the days grow shorter, trout feed actively to fatten up for the winter. Water temperatures drop, and the best fishing will usually be during the warmth of the middle of the day, much to the delight of anglers who like sleeping to a decent hour and their morning coffee. The later in the fall, and the colder the water becomes, anglers will find the fish gradually moving toward pools and feeding less avidly.

Equipment

Eight to 9 foot ultralight rods work well for Mt. Rainier and Cascade streams. While shorter rods are more appropriate to the size of the trout, a great deal of reaching, dapping, and fishing with just a small amount of fly line out beyond the rod tip is necessary, and a longer rod makes this easier.

Long leaders are preferred, at least 9 to 12 feet on larger streams, depending upon the skill of the angler. A great deal of fishing in small streams can be done with almost no or very little fly line on the water. The more leader there is on the water, the longer the drift without drag. For children, however, a shorter leader, about 7 to 9 feet, is necessary to allow them to fish efficiently.

A 6 to 7 foot leader is better for subsurface fishing, along with a weighted fly or shot 8 to 10 inches above the fly. Subsurface fishing in these streams often amounts to simply dropping a weighted fly into short runs and riffles and pools behind boulders.

While a fine tippet is not necessary, the small size of the trout and reduced visibility of finer tippets justifies using 5X to 6X for all dry fly fishing and 4X for wet fly and nymph fishing.

Fly Types

Dry flies: One almost never needs to "match the hatch" in Mt. Rainier and Cascade streams. The trout live in fast-moving water, have a limited time to eat, and usually feed opportunistically. Even if you are lucky enough to find a hatch, usually you can match it easily enough with an Adams, Wulf or Elk Hair Caddis. While anglers seldom see trout actively rising to a hatch in Cascade streams, this does not mean that the trout will not take dry flies. On the contrary, once runoff is over, anglers can have great days dry fly fishing without ever seeing a trout rise to a natural. This is probably because food is limited and the competition for it is intense.

The Adams is the most effective mayfly in these streams. Early in the season, a March Brown may be useful, and in the summer the royal families of flies, Royal Coachman, Royal Wulf, and Royal Trude, are all effective attractors.

There is no better all-around fly in the fast-moving waters of the Cascade streams than the elk hair Caddis. The elk hair is the easiest of all dry flies to fish, for it floats readily, will take trout in a variety of situations, moving slowly, fast when bouncing over riffles, when

South Cascade Brook Trout caught on ant pattern.

thrown into pockets, and frequently when it is pulled under water at the end of a drift. A Royal Wulf has most of these qualities and is a close second choice.

You do not need very many of each type of fly, i.e., two or three types of May flies, one or two types of Caddis, and some terrestrials, perhaps an ant or a stonefly.

The best dry fly size is a tossup between a 12 and a 14. A 10 is generally too big, and a 16, while often useful in slow moving water, is difficult to keep floating in fast water and hard to see. The author prefers a 12 because it is easier to fish, very visible, and often draws larger trout in the fast water than a 14 or 16.

A good floatant is absolutely essential on all Mt. Rainier and Cascade streams, as most water fished will be very fast moving and riffly.

Nymphs, wet flies, and streamers: In Mt. Rainier and Cascade streams which are affected by glacial flour and clouded up nearly all of the season, anglers must leave dry flies in their vests and use nymphs, wet flies, and streamers. Hare's Ears, Zug Bugs, and Caddis Pupae are all effective patterns, along with soft hackle flies, small Wooly Buggers, Muddler Minnows, and occasionally streamers. It is best to fish them weighted because these fast flowing streams do not allow much time to get them down to the fish. In those streams that are colored up, the most effective subsurface fishing is along the edges where the flour settles out and there is a small area of clearer water. This can mean fishing straight upstream along edges with weighted nymphs, but most often swinging the fly in toward the edges from further out in the stream.

Approaching the fish

A slow, cautious approach, fishing upstream whenever possible will yield the best results. While a few of the larger rivers require considerable walking between holding water, most do not, and once you have taken a fish or two out of a particular hole, it is time to move upstream because there are bound to be lots of good spots just ahead.

Wading is essential to the best success in fishing these streams. The shorelines are frequently too overgrown to allow effective casting. Featherweight waders are strongly recommended. They are very light and can be packed and carried by hikers efficiently. Anglers will inevitably find hip boots to be too short in too many situations.

Unless it is comparatively easy and truly necessary, fording a river will rarely result in any better fishing, for spots which require fording will seldom hold fish larger than the ones you will catch in riffles, pockets, and other likely spots reachable from a safe position.

Whitefish

Some Mt. Rainier and South Cascade streams have populations of whitefish which can be taken occasionally on the surface. Nymphs, streamers, and wet flies, all in small sizes, will take white-fish, which fight well, despite being denigrated by many fishermen.

Spin Fishing

Spin fishing, when certain practices are followed, is very much a low–impact and effective way to fish Mt. Rainier and Cascade streams and lakes. Never use triple or double hook lures—they are too hard on fish and cause an unacceptable mortality rate. There is also a tendency in spin fishing to horse fish out of the water, includ-ing reeling them right up to the rod tip. The use of reasonable drag and care of fish is essential.

Spin fishing can be particularly effective in streams when they are still running rather full and are cloudy. Many lakes are much more easily fished by spin casting than fly rod casting, particulary those with steep or heavily vegetated shorelines or shallow bottoms extending far out from shore.

South Cascade cutthroat.

Lower Skate Creek.

Ultralight or light spinning reels and rods are sufficient for Cascade trout. Four pound test line is plenty strong.

To effectively fish flies with spinning gear, the spin angler should have a few casting bubbles, the dry flies, wet flies and nymphs recommended in this book, some split shot in a variety of sizes, and some fly floatant for bubble and dry fly fishing.

Spin fishermen have a vast array of lures available. A few suggestions, particularly for lakes, are single hook flatfish and triple teasers, dick nite, brass spoons for brookie lakes and small canadian wonderspoons, all of which come with single hooks. Others, which generally have to be converted from triple or double to single hook lures, are roostertails, mepps and daredevils.

Spinners work better in streams and spoons are more effective in lakes. Across, down and back spin fishing is usually the most efficient method in streams and getting near the bottom is important. Varying retrieves is helpful in lakes.

Releasing a Fish

Hold the fish gently, avoid touching the gills or gill covers. Leave the fish in the water while removing the hook. Needlenose pliers are helpful. If the hook cannot be easily removed, cut the leader. The hook will eventually dissolve. If the fish is exhausted after the hook is removed, hold it in a swimming position in the water and move it back and forth gently, until you release it.

Appendix

... Respect for the fish's environment, in my own humble opinion, extends far beyond the water itself. It takes in all the creatures and growth under the water or on the water or along the banks. It extends far out into the countryside, into the meadows and swamps, up into the high mountains where the streams have their origin. It implies not merely a concern for such things and a desire to protect them, but a positive affection for the whole natural world and a deep desire to understand it.

Roderick Haig-Brown

Mt. Rainier National Park Regulations

It is always a good idea to call the Park to obtain updated regulations, as well as weather, trail, and fishing information. Regulations don't change as often as Mt. Rainier's weather but they do have to be adapted to changing conditions and needs. If you have selected a fishing destination, call the Park to get the latest information about access and camping at that location.

Hiking and Camping Regulations

Hiking anglers should be aware that most trails above 4,000 feet are snow-covered until at least July and bridges frequently are washed out. Water must be boiled or filtered to avoid giardia. The ten essentials should be carried along.

Wilderness Permits: Ninety-seven percent of Mt. Rainier National Park is wilderness and all camping in wilderness areas is by permit only. The number of permits is limited, and historically available on a first-come first-served basis but a reservation system is probable in the future. Check with the Park. While there are Group Wilderness Permits for group sites for 6-12 persons, no more than 5 persons are allowed at an individual site and permits must be picked up in person, up to 24 hours in advance, at: Longmire Hiker Center, Paradise Jackson Visitor Center, White River Hiker Center, Sunrise Ranger Station, Ohanapecosh Ranger Station and Carbon River Ranger Station.

Camping along trails is permitted only at the established trailside camps, all of which have designated sites, a nearby water source and toilet facilities. Cross country camping must be done only within cross country zones, must be at least 0.25 miles from any road or established trail and at least 100 feet from lakes, streams and wetlands. Alpine hiking, above the tree line and in established Alpine zones, is permitted only on permanent snow or ice or on bare ground previously used as campsites. There are three camping areas for autos within the park.

Prohibited activities on trails and back country: Fires, except stoves; pets; bicycle use on trails; all weapons; destroying or disturbing any natural, cultural, or archeological feature; feeding, disturbing, or hunting wildlife; shortcutting on any trail; polluting or contaminating any water source; disposing of human waste within 100 feet of water or within sight of a trail; camping within 100 feet of water except in a designated campsite. All trash must be packed out and no-trace practices should always be the rule.

National Forest Wilderness Regulations

The Wilderness areas surrounding Mt. Rainier National Park are managed by the United States Department of Agriculture Forest Service. There are general Wilderness regulations applicable to all of the areas and some specific regulations in each Wilderness area. For specific information, contact the District Ranger Offices listed in the appendix. The regulations are designed to protect natural resources and to preserve the opportunity for solitude promised by the Wilderness Act. The general regulations of particular importance to anglers are the following:

Prohibited activities: Possessing or using a motor vehicle, motorboat or motorized equipment; possessing or using a bicycle; shortcutting a trail switchback; camping within 100 feet of the shoreline of any lake; and camping within 100 feet of the Pacific Crest Trail.

Permits: Permits are required in some of the Wilderness areas and not in others. Inquire at District Ranger Station. Groups are limited to 12 people.

Using the No Trace Ethic

Increasing populations near Mt. Rainier National Park and the South Cascade mountains have resulted in expanding use of the Park and surrounding forest areas. The good news is that visitors are far more conscious of what is popularly described as the "no-trace ethic" and are incorporating it into their actions. The fundamental values of this ethic are as follows.

Group Size: Limit your group size while hiking and camping, as smaller groups have less impact on the land.

Travel: Do not shortcut established trail switchbacks. Staying on the trail prevents erosion. When traveling off established trails, watch where you step, especially above timberline where plant life is fragile and easily destroyed.

Finding a Campsite: Choose an area which will allow you to leave it without any trace of your use. Locate an area which does not require leveling; in a wooded area on bare ground or forest litter at least 200 feet away from lakes and streams; away from trails and main areas of attraction; with several available routes to and from camp to minimize damage to soils and plants.

Campfires: In many forest areas, campfires are not allowed. It is far preferable to use a portable stove. If campfires are allowed, never cut live or standing dead trees. Always use existing fire-rings if available; otherwise, clear the ground to soil. Do not line with rocks and keep away from logs, roots, brush and tree trunks. Keep the fire small. When the fire is not needed, drown and stir it, with a stick or trowel. Be sure that the fire is dead out, then bury the ashes and return the area to its natural state before leaving.

Sanitation

Dig a small hole 6 inches deep and at least 200 feet from water, trails or campsites, bury human waste and toilet paper, replace the soil, and restore the site as nearly as possible. Carry water to the campsite for washing and bathing. Avoid using soap, using biodegradable soap when necessary. Dispose of waste water well away from lakes and streams.

Leave No Trace

Pack out everything you carried in. Place all trash in a litter bag, including plastic, cans, tinfoil, and leftover food items. Don't burn or bury any of these items. Carry out every kind of litter, including anything left by others. Restore the area to its natural state.

Fishing Regulations and Licenses

Mt. Rainier National Park

License, Regulations and Seasons: Park rules are subject to change at any time. Contact the Park for updated rules. No fishing license is required inside the Park. Park fishing seasons are designed to accord with regulations set by the Washington Department of Fish and Wildlife for the surrounding areas. Thus, opening and closing dates for lakes, ponds and streams correspond to those set by the State. In general, Washington State's freshwater fishing regulations allow fishing in lakes and ponds year around, with many specific exceptions, and streams open for fishing June 1, closing October 31. Specific Park rules control gear and limits, and there are specific closures. The Park's rules are available at any entrance gate.

Prohibited Activities: Possession or use of live or dead bait, amphibians, non-preserved fish eggs, or roe; fish stocking, chumming or placing any substance in waters for the purpose of attracting or feeding fish; fishing with nets, seines, traps, drugs or explosives, or any means other than hook and line with the rod or line being closely attended; digging for bait; placing refuse of any kind in any park waters.

Fly Fishing Only: The Ohanapecosh River and its tributaries, including Ollallie Creek, Panther Creek, Boulder Creek, Deer Creek, Kotsuck Creek, and Chinook Creek, are open to fly fishing only. Bait and other artificial lures are prohibited.

Closed Waters: Klickitat Creek above the White River entrance water supply intake. Ipsut Creek above the Ipsut Creek campground water supply intake. Laughingwater Creek above the Ohanapecosh water supply intake. Frozen Lakes, Reflection Lakes, Shadow Lake, Tipsoo Lake.

Barbless hooks and artificial lures are not required but are encouraged as is catch and release, especially in the streams and in lakes with cutthroat and rainbow populations. The Park Service encourages taking a limit of brook trout from the Park's lakes.

All bull trout must be released. The bull trout is a threatened species and may be placed upon the endangered species list.

South Cascades

Outside the Park, a Washington State freshwater fishing license is required and regulations are established by the State. The license is not sold inside the Park but is sold in most hardware and sporting goods stores in the area. Just as it is required inside the Park, all bull trout must be released.

Catch and Release

When fishing in Mt. Rainier National Park and the South Cascade Mountains, use barbless hooks and practice catch and release, unless fishing lakes which have stocked fish or eastern brook and you plan to eat them. It is recommended that bait not be used when fishing any Park lakes that contain rainbow and cutthroat because continued existence of these species within the Park's lakes is solely dependant upon sufficient numbers of fish surviving and spawning. Do not use bait when fishing the rivers and creeks, as the trout populations are limited and fragile. This is especially important in the rivers which contain bull trout.

Useful Information

Telephone Numbers

Mt. Rainier National Park Information: 360-569-2211.
   Homepage address: www.nps.gov/mora/
Washington Department of Fish & Wildlife (lake and stream
   information outside the Park): 360-902-2200

Entrance fees to Mt. Rainier National Park

Fees are charged per vehicle at White River, Carbon River, Nisqually, and Stevens Canyon entrances. All other access is free.

Weather

It is always advisable to call the Park for weather information. Depending upon the amount of winter snowfall, much of the Park is inaccessible until at least early summer. Once summer arrives in earnest, high temperatures average in the high sixties and low seventies, cooling 20-30 degrees and more at night. Summer is generally very pleasant but Mt. Rainier creates its own weather to an extent and anglers should always have heavy clothing and rain gear readily available. Temperatures decline in the fall, rain becomes more frequent but much of the season is dry and offers good fishing opportunities through September and even into October in some years. Sudden storms occur and all visitors should be prepared.

Lodging

Within the Park, only National Park Inn at Longmire and Paradise Inn have overnight accomodations. Reservations must be made very early for both at 360-569-2275.

Outside the Park, there are motels, cabins, inns and other lodging available. Reservations are a good idea, particularly when seeking to stay overnight close to one of the Park's entrances.

Ranger Stations

Rangers are the best sources of information about access, weather, fishing, camping, hiking and specific areas inside and outside the Park.

North: White River District, 857 Roosevelt E., Enumclaw, WA, 360-825-6585.

South: Randle Ranger District, Randle, WA 98377, 360-497-7565. Packwood Ranger District, Packwood WA 98361, 360-494-5515.

East: Naches Ranger District, Naches, WA 98397, 509-653-2205.

Fly Fishing Shops

Sports Hut, P.O. Box 282, Packwood, WA, 360-494-7321.
The Morning Hatch, 3630 Cedar, Tacoma, WA, 206-472-1070.
Clearwater Angler, 620 Auburn Way, Auburn WA, 206-939-1484.
Gary's Fly Shop, 1210 W. Lincoln, Yakima, WA, 509-457-3474.
The Fly Fisher, 5622 Pacific Ave SE, Lacey, WA, 360-491-0181.

Topographic Maps and Guidebooks

Anglers will find topographic maps and hiking guidebooks a necessity, not an option, for most fishing in Mt. Rainier National Park and the surrounding South Cascade mountains.

Guidebooks

50 Hikes in Mt. Rainier National Park, Ira Spring, Mountaineers, Seattle, WA, 3rd Ed. 1988.

Adventure Guide to Mt. Rainier, Jeff Smoot, Chockstone Press, Evergreen Colorado, 1991.

100 Hikes in Washington's South Cascades and Olympics, Ira Spring and Harvey Manning, Mountaineers, Seattle, WA, 1992.

Best Short Hikes in Washington's South Cascades and Olympics, E.M. Sterling, Mountaineers, Seattle, WA, 1995.

Pacific Northwest Hiking, Ron Judd and Dan Nelson, Foghorn Press, San Francisco, CA, 1995.

Topographic Maps

Mt. Rainier National Park Visitors Guide provides a basic map of the Park and its roads and trails.

More detail of the Park and the surrounding National Forest and Wilderness areas is provided by *Green Trails* maps, PO box 1272, Bellevue, WA 98009.

The National Forest Service provides good topographic maps of National Forest and Wilderness Areas. Particularly useful are maps of William O. Douglas Wilderness and Norse Peak Wilderness.

Campgrounds

West

Carbon River

Ipsut Creek: 5 mi. inside RNP from Carbon River Entrance. 29 sites for tent/RV. Water. Fee.

Mowich Lake

Evans Creek : Rd. 7920 off Mowich Lake Road, 1.5 mi to campground. 27 tent sites, water. No fee.

Mowich Lake: At the end of Mowich Lake Road. Very limited sites.

Nisqually River

Sunshine Point: RNP. Within one mile of Nisqually Entrance RNP. 18 sites for tent/RV. Water. Fee.

Longmire/Paradise

Cougar Rock:2 mi. past Longmire on the road to Paradise. 200 tent/RV sites. Water. Fee.

South

Cispus River

Iron Creek: South of Randle on Highway 131 for 1 mi., then Rd. 25 for 9 mi.. On Cispus River. 98 sites for tent/RV. Water. Fee. Partial reservations.800-280-CAMP.

Tower Rock: South of Randle on Highway 131 one mile, then Rd. 23 6.5 mi., south on Rd. 28, then Rd. 76. 22 sites tent/RV. On Cispus River. Fee.

North Fork: Rd. 23 11 mi. from Highway 131. 33 sites for tent/RV. Water. Fee. On North Fork Cispus River.

Blue Lake Creek: 4 mi. past North Fork campground on Rd. 23. 11 sites for tent/RV. Water. Fee.

Packwood

La Wis Wis: 7 mi. east of Packwood on Highway 12, then Rd. 1272 .4 mile. 100 sites tent/RV. Water. Fee.

East

Ohanapecosh

Ohanapecosh RNP: 5 mi. north on Cayuse Pass Highway 123 from Highway 12. 205 sites tent/RV. Fee. On Ohanapecosh River.

Summit Creek: 10 mi. east of Packwood on Highway 12, then north on Rd. 45, to 4510 for 7 mi.. 7 tent sites. No water. No fee. On Summit Creek.

Soda Springs: 4 mi. beyond Summit Creek Campground on Rd. 4510. 8 tent sites. No Water. No fee. On Summit Creek.

White Pass

White Pass Lake: 19 mi. east of Packwood on Highway 12. 16 sites for tent/RV. No Water. No fee. On Leech Lake.

Dog Lake: 3 mi. east of White Pass Lake Campground on Highway 12. 11 sites for tent/RV. No water. No fee. On Dog Lake.

Clear Lake South: 35 mi. west of Naches on Highway 12, then south on Rd. 1200 one mile. 23 sites tent/RV. Water. No fee.

Clear Lake North: .5 mile south of Clear Lake South Campground on Rd. 840. 35 sites tent/RV. On Clear Lake. Fee

South Fork: Drive Rd. 1200 3 mi. past Clear Lake South Campground, then west .5 mile on Rd. 1382. 15 sites tent/RV. No water. No fee. On South Fork Tieton River.

Indian Creek: 31.5 mi. west of Naches on Highway 12. 39 sites tent/RV. Water. Fee. On Rinrock Lake.

Peninsula: 2 mi. past Clear Lake South campground on Rd. 1200, then west on 1382 one mile to lake. 19 sites tent/RV. No fee. On Rimrock Lake.

American River

Lodge Pole: East of Chinook Pass 7 mi. from RNP on Highway 410. 32 sites tent/RV. Water. Fee. On the American River.

Pleasant Valley: Approximately 3 mi. east of Lodge Pole campground off Highway 410. 26 sites tent/RV. Water. Fee. On the American River.

Hell's Crossing: .5 mi. east of Pleasant Valley Campground off Highway 410. 18 sites tent/RV. Water. Fee. On American River.

Little Naches River

Little Naches: Immediately up Rd. 1900, Little Naches River Road, off Highway 410. 21 sites tent/RV. Water. Fee.

Kaner Flat: 2.5 mi. up Rd. 1900 off Highway 410. 49 sites tent/RV. Water. Fee.

Crow Creek: Take Rd. 1902 from 1900 off Highway 410. 15 sites tentrings. Rd. 2000 off of Highway 410, 5 mi. to campground. 26 sites tent/RV. Water. Fee. On Bumping River.

Cougar Flat: One mile toward Bumping Lake from Soda Springs campground. 9 sites tent/RV. Water. Fee. On Bumping River.

Bumping Crossing: About one mile from east end of Bumping Lake. No water. No fee. On Bumping River.

Bumping Lake: At Bumping Lake. 50 sites tent/RV. Water. Fee.

North

Greenwater

The Dalles: Adjacent to Highway 410 15 mi. north from entrance to RNP. 19 tent sites, 26 tent/RV. Water. Partial reservations 800-280-CAMP

Corral Pass: 6 mi. on Rd. 7174 off Highway 410. No trailers or RV. 20 tent site. No Water. No fee.

Silver Springs: 9 mi. north from entrance to RNP on Highway 410. 16 tent sites. 40 tent/RV sites. Water. Fee. Partial reservations. 800-280-CAMP.

White River Entrance RNP

White River RNP: 7 mi. on White River Road from entrance to RNP. 117 sites tent/RV. Water. Fee.

Sources

Bradner, Enos *Northwest Angling* Binford & Morts, Portland Ore. 1969.

Douglas, Wm O. *My Wilderness*, Doubleday & Co. New York , 1960.

Douglas, Wm. O. *Of Men and Mountains* , Chronicle Books, San Francisco 1990.

Filley, Bette *The Fact Book About Mt. Rainier*, Dunamis House, Issaquah, WA, 1996.

A Primer of Fly Fishing Roderick Haig-Brown, Amato Publications Portland, OR, 1964.

Jones, Stan *Washington State Fishing Guide*, Stan Jones Publishing Co. Seattle, WA, 1995.

Judd, Ron and Nelson, Dan A. *Pacific Northwest Hiking*, Foghorn Press, San Francisco, Cal. 1995.

Smoot, Jeff *Adventure Guide to Mt. Rainier*, Chockstone Press, Evergreen Colorado, 1991.

Spring, Ira and Harvey Manning *100 Hikes in Washington's South Cascades and Olympics* Mountaineers, Seattle, WA, 1992.

Spring, Ira *50 Hikes in Mt. Rainier National Park*, Mountaineers, Seattle, WA, 3rd Ed. 1988.

Sterling, E.M. *Best Short Hikes in Washington's South Cascades and Olympics*, Mountaineers, Seattle, WA, 1995.

A Year in Paradise, Floyd Schmoe, 1922 Mountaineers, Seattle, WA.

Alpine Lake Survey Report Yakima County WDFW , Mark Deleray and Cindra Barbee, 1991.

Alpine Lake Surveys, Gifford Pinchot and Snoqualmie National Forests, WDFW.

Alpine Lake Surveys Lewis County, WDFW.

Mount Rainier, A Record of Exploration, Edmond S. Meany, 1906 Binford &Mort, Portland, OR

"The Best Fishing in America," Ted Trueblood, *Field and Stream Magazine,* 1959.

"Wait a Minute," Fred Everett, *Field & Stream Magazine*, 1937.

Index